Co

Co

SCIENTIFIC
AMERICAN *SOURCEBOOKS*

ENDANGERED
MAMMALS OF
NORTH AMERICA

VICTORIA SHERROW

 TWENTY-FIRST CENTURY BOOKS

A Division of Henry Holt and Company
New York

For my daughter, Christine, with love

ACKNOWLEDGMENTS

The author is grateful to the following organizations for their assistance during the preparation of this book: Arizona Game and Fish Department, Bat Conservation International, Florida Department of Natural Resources, Greater Yellowstone Coalition, Save the Manatee Club, and Florida Power & Light Company. (Maps on pp. 14, 17, and 84 are based on materials provided by FP&L.)

Twenty-First Century Books / A Division of Henry Holt and Company, Inc. / *Publishers since 1866*
115 West 18th Street / New York, NY 10011

Henry Holt® and colophon are trademarks of Henry Holt and Company, Inc.

Henry Holt and Company, Inc., and Scientific American, Inc., are both wholly owned subsidiaries of Holtzbrinck Publishing Holdings Limited Partnership. Twenty-First Century Books, a division of Henry Holt and Company, Inc., is using the Scientific American name under a special license with that company.

The maps featured in this book were created by Sandee Cohen.

Library of Congress Cataloging-in-Publication Data

Sherrow, Victoria / Endangered mammals of North America / Victoria Sherrow. — 1st ed.
p. cm. — (Scientific American sourcebooks). Includes bibliographical references (p.) and index.
1. Rare mammals—North America—Juvenile literature. 2. Endangered species—North America—Juvenile literature. 3. Wildlife conservation—North America—Juvenile literature.
[1.Endangered species. 2. Rare animals. 3. Mammals. 4. Wildlife conservation.] I. Title. II. Series.
QL706.83.N7S48 1995   599'.0042'097—dc20   95–940

ISBN 0–8050–3253–3 (hardcover) / ISBN 0–8050–3252–5 (paperback)
First Edition 1995

Printed in Mexico.
10 9 8 7 6 5 4 3 2

Photo Credits

pp. 10, 68: Z. Leszczynski/Animals Animals; p. 13: U.S. Fish and Wildlife Service Photo by Gaylen Rathburn; p. 16: James D. Watt/Animals Animals; p. 18: H. K. Management, Inc.; p. 20: David J. Rugh/National Marine Mammal Laboratory; p. 22: Flip Nicklin/Minden Pictures; p. 25: National Marine Mammal Laboratory; p. 26: Larry Foster/EarthViews; pp. 30, 33, 34, 37, 38: Bob Miles/Arizona Game and Fish Dept.; pp. 40, 43, 44, 49, 50: Merlin D. Tuttle; p. 52: Thomas Kitchin/Tom Stack and Associates; p. 54: Robert Winslow/Tom Stack and Associates; p. 56: Joe McDonald/Animals Animals; p. 61: Dewey Vanderhoff; p. 64: Jim Tuten/Animals Animals; p. 66: Barbara von Hoffman/Tom Stack and Associates; p. 69: Reed/Williams/Animals Animals; p. 71: U.S. Fish and Wildlife Service Photo by Luray Parker/Wyoming Fish and Game; p. 73: North Wind Picture Archives; p. 75: Stouffer Prod./Animals Animals; p. 77: Nancy Adams/Tom Stack and Associates; p. 78: John Pontier/Animals Animals; p. 81: Maresa Pryor/Animals Animals; p. 83: R. Overton/Florida Department of Commerce, Division of Tourism.

CONTENTS

LIFE ON A CHANGING PLANET

*L*ooking at North America today, we get only glimpses of how the land looked thousands of years ago. Most of it was wilderness, often thickly forested or carpeted with miles of uninterrupted grasslands on the prairies and plains. The continent, which includes present-day Canada, the United States, and Mexico, gradually developed a mosaic of landforms—hills, mountains, basins, and flatlands—sprigged with lakes, rivers, and other waters. The climate ranged from the arctic chill of northern Canada, Alaska, and Greenland to the tropical heat of southern Mexico, allowing for a rich variety of vegetation and wildlife.

Scientists think the first living organisms emerged on earth around 3.5 billion years ago. Many types of animals have come and gone during these millennia. We know little about some of them. Others, such as dinosaurs, have been studied intensely although they became extinct, or died out, about 65 million years ago.

Mammals, the class of animals that includes humankind, first appeared on earth about 225 to 190 million years ago, during what is called the Triassic period of history. Although this group includes such different creatures as squirrels, bats, wolves, kangaroos, zebras, and whales, mammals share many traits. All are vertebrates (animals with backbones) and all have a cranium (a hard case made of bone or cartilage that encases the brain). Most bear live young, and all feed their young milk made in the mother's body.

Mammals also have hair, which may be thick or thin, coarse or soft. Hair protects them and provides warmth. Sensory hairs (whiskers) on the cheeks, lips, or head can help an animal feel its way around in the dark. Eyebrows and lashes keep dirt out of the eyes. All hairy animals are mammals, yet not all mammals have a lot of hair. For example, whales have only a few bristles on their chins and snouts.

As warm-blooded animals, mammals maintain body temperatures that are within a narrow range all the time. This means they can survive in a wide range of climates and in changing temperatures. Since mammals need more fuel to stay active in harsh weather, they eat more food than do cold-blooded animals. Their body systems are designed for efficiency. Powered by a four-chambered heart, a mammal's circulating blood carries more oxygen than does the blood of other animals.

VANISHING SPECIES   Since mammals first appeared on earth, more species have arisen and become extinct than the total number now living. Extinction is a natural part of life. Throughout history, numerous mammal species have become extinct. They died out over the course of many years because of predators, a lack of food, or other conditions to which they could not adapt. Some mammals are especially vulnerable because of their large size or highly specialized diet. Or they may have been scarce to begin with. Changes in climate, natural disasters, or disease can also wipe out a species.

In North America during the Stone Age, there were millions of woolly mammoths, giant sloths, long-horned bison, and saber-toothed cats. These mammals had become extinct by 6500 B.C. In modern times, species are dying out far more rapidly than they did in the past. Scientists believe that for millions of years, only one or two species of plants or animals became extinct each year. Yet in recent decades, extinctions have become so frequent that in 1992, about 365 species (an average of one a day) became extinct, meaning they have not been seen in the wild for at least fifty years.

In modern times, animals have died out because a growing human population has destroyed their habitats or killed and used them in large numbers. Human technology, growing steadily since the industrial revolution that began in England during the late 1700s, has upset the balance of nature. Centuries of hunting, fishing, and clearing of land, along with air and water pollution, have diminished animals and their habitats—the places where they live.

As a result, many animals are struggling to survive. Unprecedented numbers of mammals, as well as birds, reptiles, and amphibians, now face extinction. More than a thousand species are endangered—in immediate danger of extinction in some or all parts of their range. Other species are threatened—plentiful in some areas but declining in total numbers. Hundreds of other species are considered rare. They have such small populations that they need much help to survive.

◆ HOW LIVING THINGS ARE CLASSIFIED ◆

In order to identify and study living things, scientists rely on a universal system of naming and classifying them. That way, people from anywhere in the world can be sure they are referring to the same organism for purposes of labeling, study, or discussion. The science of classifying animals and plants is called taxonomy. The modern classification system used in biology is based on the work of Carolus Linnaeus (1707–1778), a Swedish botanist (a scientist who studies plants). Using the system, biologists identify, name, and group organisms with those that share their important traits so that they can be distinguished from others that are different. The system also reveals something about the evolution of a particular organism.

The broadest categories used in taxonomy are the kingdoms—animal and plant, for instance. Kingdoms are further divided into other categories, including phylum, class, order, family, genus, and species. The species is considered to be the most basic of all these categories. There are several million different species of organisms.

In practice, the system works like this: a bowhead whale belongs to the animal kingdom and to the phylum Chordata; class Mammalia; order Cetacea; family Balaenidae; genus *Balaena*; and species *mysticetus*.

SEVEN CHIEF GROUPS MAKE UP THE SYSTEM OF TAXONOMY, OR SCIENTIFIC CLASSIFICATION:

KINGDOM

PHYLUM

CLASS

ORDER

FAMILY

GENUS

SPECIES

An animal's scientific name combines the name of its genus and its species. Sometimes the name of its subspecies is included, as well.

LOST HABITATS   A major cause of extinction today is a loss of animal habitats through deforestation (the cutting down of trees) and the destruction of wetlands. A growing human population uses ever more land and resources. Caribbean manatees and Florida panthers are among the animals that have declined for this reason.

At one time, nearly one-half of the earth was covered with forests. Only one-fifth of them remain. Logging has reduced North American forests considerably, with a 90 percent decrease in conifer woods (firs, spruce, hemlocks, pines, larch, and others) in the northwest United States. In Canada during the early 1990s, forests were being cut at a rate exceeding deforestation in the tropical rain forest. One section that was heavily cut was the vast forest of spruce, aspen, and birch that stretches from the Yukon to Labrador. This has reduced the habitats of the great gray owl and barren-ground caribou, among others.

Growing human populations have often drained wetlands and used grassy or shrubbed lands as grazing areas for livestock. Woodlands have made way for homes and roads, leaving wild animals with smaller areas that cannot support as many inhabitants. Isolated from others of their own kind, these animals have trouble finding mates. Mating within small groups means mating between animals that are genetically similar. This often results in offspring that are less adaptable than are animals that inherit more diverse sets of genes.

OTHER THREATS   Besides destroying their habitats, a growing human population has killed many animals, such as certain kinds of whales, for commercial reasons. Other animals have died out when new diseases or predators were brought into their environments. Planned "pest control," such as attempts to reduce the number of prairie dogs, has endangered black-footed ferrets, which depend on the prairie dogs for food.

Human activities release toxins into the environment. Many pesticides and fertilizers leave residues in soil, water, and food. Factory and car-exhaust fumes contaminate the air. Speaking of this, ecologist Barry Commoner calls people born after the 1940s "a generation with DDT [dichloro-diphenyl-trichloroethane] in their fat [and] carbon monoxide and lead in their bones." Chemicals such as DDT and PCBs (polychlorinated biphenyls) have polluted the water and soil, harming living things. When plants and animals at the bottom of the food chain are poisoned, that affects many others. Smaller animals are eaten by larger animals, which in turn are eaten by still larger animals, spreading the poison up the food chain. Pollution can damage an animal's health and reproductive system so that it produces abnormal offspring or none at all.

PROTECTIVE EFFORTS   Slowly, people have come to realize that while humans have the ability to exploit the environment, inventing tools and devices that help us to thrive, many animals and plants are at our mercy. There has been a growing effort to protect the earth's natural resources and living things.

These efforts have come both from government and private citizens. Early in the 1900s, laws were passed to protect some endangered wildlife from commercial trade and too much hunting. In 1973, Congress passed the Endangered Species Act. Its goal was to conserve the ecosystems on which endangered species depend and to discourage the killing of these species in all countries. The landmark 1973 law states that endangered animals may not be "killed, hunted, collected, harassed, harmed, pursued, shot, trapped, wounded, or captured." The United States also signed formal agreements with Canada, Mexico, and other nations to protect migratory birds.

In 1975, the Convention on International Trade in Endangered Species of Wild Flora and Fauna (CITES) was ratified by ninety-six nations and signed by the United States. This law makes it a crime to sell or transport an endangered species or any products made from them. It contains specific bans on the importation and trade of such products.

The Endangered Species Act recognizes certain crucial habitats and sets them aside to promote the survival of various endangered species. The United States government is forbidden to use such lands in ways that would harm endangered species, but private use of these lands is not always banned. This has led to ongoing conflicts between businesses and environmental groups. In addition, state and local governments have discretion in interpreting the laws and deciding when and how to act in enforcing them. And some people simply break the laws, continuing to hunt endangered animals for sport or profit.

Hard choices must be made for both the short and the long term as people decide how much land, money, and effort will be devoted to wildlife preservation. Recent discussions have focused on ways to balance property rights with the preservation of nature. Federal agencies have been considering proposals that would compensate property owners for any income lost as a result of the Endangered Species Act.

Conservationists have increasingly pointed out the importance of early intervention to save different species. This means planning and working to save species while they are still common rather than waiting until they become endangered. Experts point out that many of today's endangered species were common two or three decades ago.

Another approach is to focus on promoting the health of whole ecosystems instead of focusing on just one type of plant or animal. Conservationists who want to revise the Endangered Species Act say that focusing on prevention and using an ecosystemwide approach would strengthen the act.

In the meantime, a number of North American mammals are in danger of extinction. The following chapters describe the conditions of just a few of these mammals and the efforts that are being made to help them survive.

ONE

GENTLE WATER GIANTS
CARIBBEAN MANATEES

A visitor to Florida's lakes and rivers will soon notice signs warning CAUTION—MANATEE AREA. Aluminum sculptures of manatees remind boat operators that the massive, grayish brown creatures are moving about underwater.

In a 1988 report, the U.S. Marine Mammal Commission called the Caribbean manatee, or sea cow (*Trichechus manatus*), one of the most endangered marine mammals in North America's coastal waters. There may be only about 1,800 manatees left. They do not harm other species and have no natural enemies, but collisions with commercial and recreational boats kill some every year. Since the 1970s, laws and programs to educate the public have aimed to save the manatee.

◆ ◆ ◆

The manatee is a huge but harmless creature that can reach a length of 13 feet (4 meters) and weigh up to 3,500 pounds (1,600 kilograms). The average adult manatee is 10 feet (3 meters) long and weighs from 800 to 1,200 pounds (360 to 544 kilograms). Their streamlined bodies end in rounded tails. They lack hind limbs and have flexible, short front limbs with three or four nails on the tip of each flipper.

The manatee's small eyes are set wide apart in its bulbous face, giving it a distinctive, peaceful appearance. Tiny ear openings can be found just behind the eyes. Stiff whiskers sprout around their faces, and other hairs are scattered sparsely across their taut, rough hides. Flexible upper lips enable them to move their food—hydrilla, water hyacinths, and other vegetation from the water—into their mouths. People who have touched a manatee's snout say it feels soft, like deerskin.

CARIBBEAN MANATEE
Trichechus manatus

KINGDOM: Animalia

PHYLUM: Chordata

CLASS: Mammalia

ORDER: Sirenia

FAMILY: Trichechidae

GENUS: *Trichechus*

SPECIES: *manatus*

As manatees move slowly through the water, their streamlined bodies may be hard to spot until they surface for air. A soft swirling occurs on the water as they emerge. Large manatees can stay underwater fifteen to twenty minutes at a time; smaller ones must come up for air perhaps twice as often.

Although normally quiet, manatees occasionally make sounds resembling squeals, chirps, and whistles. They seem to use these sounds to communicate, when a calf squeaks for its mother, for example. Manatees vocalize when they are mating or playing or when they are frightened. They may also greet new arrivals with a rapid string of noises.

After mating, the male manatee, called a bull, leaves. The female is pregnant for twelve to thirteen months and then finds a quiet place to give birth. A single calf is usually born in the spring or summer. Newborns weigh about 66 pounds (30 kilograms) and are 4 to 4.5 feet (1.2 to 1.4 meters) long.

Apparently, calves swim soon after birth. They suckle milk from their mother's nipples, located near the "armpit" area of her front flipper. Although calves can eat on their own after a year, they stay with their mothers for about two years. A calf swims alongside its mother behind her flipper. (Otherwise manatees tend to swim single file.) Females fiercely protect their young, swimming between them and any humans or animals that approach.

Among manatees, a female and her calf are the basic social unit. A mother shows her calf where the feeding places are and the routes to and from warm-water areas. During colder months, manatee herds congregate in large groups in warmer waters.

Manatees are playful. Some have been seen "body surfing" on currents of water in a parallel formation. Between rides they drift, nuzzle one another, and make noises. Another of their games resembles "follow the leader." One or more animals will follow a "leader," mimicking his or her actions, such as diving and turning.

Manatee calves live on their mothers' milk for about a year.

The manatee's normal life span in the wild is uncertain, but one captive in a Florida aquarium has passed the age of forty. Scientists believe manatees may live to be fifty to seventy years of age.

AN ANCIENT MARINE MAMMAL

Manatees are ancient, having evolved millions of years ago from land mammals. They belong to the order Sirenia, from the Latin word *sirens*. The Sirens were mythical sea nymphs who tried to lure Greek heroes into perilous waters. Once sirenians were varied and numerous. Now there are only four types: three species of manatee and the dugong, which lives in the Pacific.

At one time people thought manatees were related to walruses because of their faces. But their bodies, habitats, and ancestry are quite different from those of the walrus. Scientists discovered a common ancestry with the same group of animals that later produced elephants. These ancestors lived around thirty-five million years ago, probably in Africa and Eurasia. Some migrated to the Caribbean and North America. Long ago, sailors thought manatees were mermaids. Christopher Columbus spotted some manatees off the coast of Haiti in 1493 and wrote in his ship's log that they were not as lovely as he had expected, but "to some extent they have a human appearance in the face."

A WARM-WATER RANGE   The Caribbean manatee lives in warm tropical and subtropical waters, either fresh or salt—rivers, estuaries, and coastal areas. These waters are fairly shallow; they are not deep oceans. During the summer months, manatees range as far north as Virginia and as

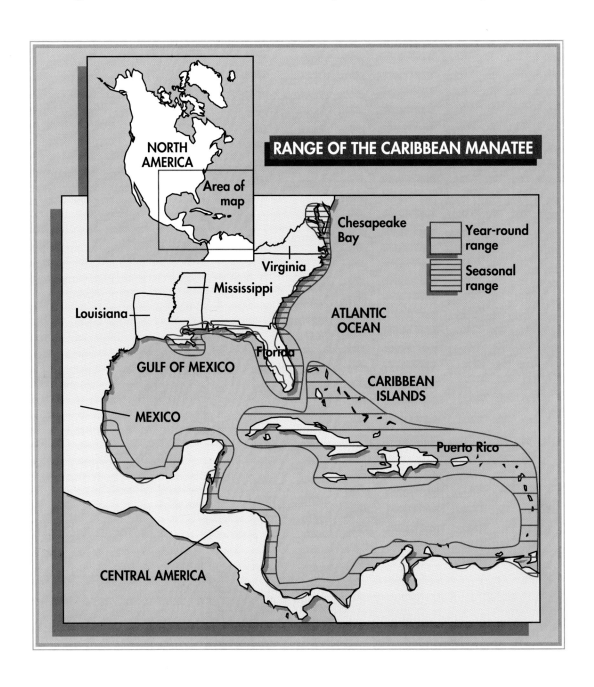

far west as Mississippi and Louisiana. Year-round, some stay close to peninsular Florida and southern Georgia, while others live in Bahamian waters. They move along the Atlantic coast, from St. John's River in northeastern Florida southward to the Miami area; and on the Gulf coast, they move around the shores of Everglades National Park. Manatees also live in the waters off Mexico and Central America.

There these herbivores (plant-eating animals) find sea grasses and other plants to eat. Large adult manatees may consume more than 200 pounds (90 kilograms) of vegetation each day. This represents from 5 to 10 percent of their body weight. They spend about one-fourth of each day eating.

DWINDLING NUMBERS   Centuries ago people hunted manatees for their delicious meat and fat for cooking. Manatees were an occasional food—though not a staple—for the Maya of Mexico, aboriginal peoples of Florida, and others on the southern North American coast. Manatee hides were used to make shields, whips, and other goods; manatee bones were carved into tools and weapons. When white Europeans arrived in Florida in the 1400s, the Seminoles traded manatee meat with them. White explorers, settlers, and missionaries saw and wrote about how manatees were hunted with spears.

Hunting manatees was banned in 1972, but unusually cold weather is an ongoing threat to them. When the water grows too cold, they may stop feeding, use up their body fat to stay warm, and become dehydrated. Young manatees die faster from cold than do adults. In 1990, about forty-four manatees died off the Florida coast because of cold weather. Apparently they could not swim to a warmer area in time to save themselves.

The current major threats to manatees are habitat destruction and collisions with boats. During the 1900s, more people moved to coastal areas. They built homes, farms, and citrus groves, resulting in a loss of manatee habitats and food. Between 1950 and 1975, about 72,000 acres (28,800 hectares) of wetlands were destroyed in Florida every year. And in the 1990s, the state's human population continues to increase by about 1,000 people daily.

On the water, fishing and boating are the major threats to manatees. Their flippers become entangled in crab-pot lines and other fishing gear. Speedboats kill some and injure others. By the 1990s, there were an estimated 500,000 commercial and recreational boats in Florida. Veterinarian Jesse

Because manatees swim in shallow waters, they are often injured by boat propellers.

R. White explains, "The propellers of freighters and barge-towing tugs can cut a manatee almost in half."

Manatees usually swim too slowly to escape harm from boats. Between 1976 and 1993, most manatee deaths (including nursing calves that lost their mothers) were watercraft-related. The birthrate, which declined from the 1970s to the 1990s, has not kept up with the death rate. By 1991, there were about 1,800 manatees left, and many people feared they would be extinct by the year 2000.

CONSERVATION EFFORTS   Efforts to save the manatee have united federal and state agencies, power-plant operators, oceanariums, conservationists, and private citizens. Since 1970, legislation has given the Florida Department of Natural Resources both funds and the authority to protect manatees and their habitats. The Florida Manatee Sanctuary Act of 1978 offered more protection. Safe manatee habitats were set aside. These places contain vegetation, fresh water for drinking, and a warm-water source in the winter.

Since manatees like water that is at least 70°F (21°C), they gravitate to the water around the outflow pipes near the power plants that serve Florida residents. There are six or more sources of warm water year-round on the East Coast—five power-plant outflows and one natural spring. The power plants provide warm-water refuges for manatees and have emergency plans for times when a plant shuts down unexpectedly, leaving the animals in cold water.

The federal Marine Mammal Protection Act of 1972 and the

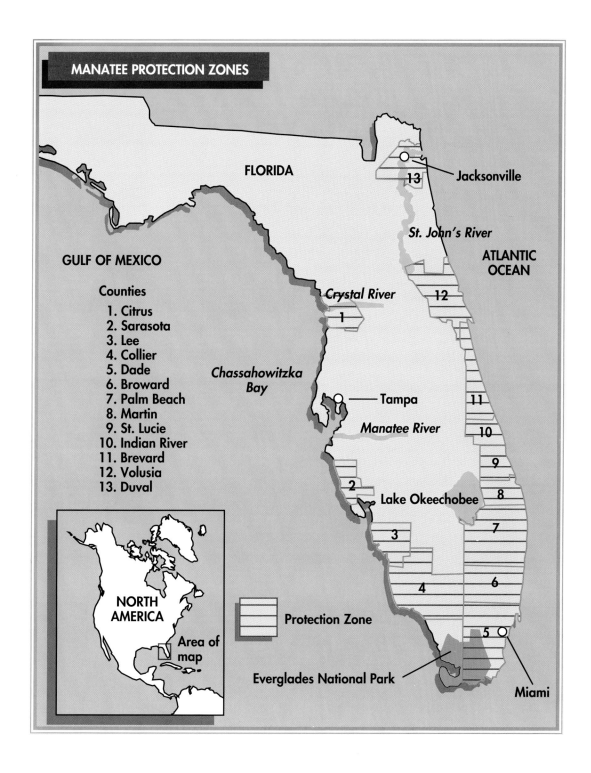

MANATEE PROTECTION ZONES

FLORIDA

Jacksonville

St. John's River

GULF OF MEXICO

ATLANTIC OCEAN

Counties
1. Citrus
2. Sarasota
3. Lee
4. Collier
5. Dade
6. Broward
7. Palm Beach
8. Martin
9. St. Lucie
10. Indian River
11. Brevard
12. Volusia
13. Duval

Crystal River

Chassahowitzka Bay

Tampa

Manatee River

Lake Okeechobee

NORTH AMERICA

Area of map

Protection Zone

Everglades National Park

Miami

Endangered Species Act of 1973 aided manatees by making those who kill, injure, capture, or harass an endangered animal subject to prison or a $20,000 fine. But some people simply break the law. In 1988, two butchered manatees were found in Florida waters.

The Florida Manatee Recovery Plan, developed in 1980, set up a recov-

ery team to reduce manatee deaths, especially from boating. Boat speeds were restricted in certain areas, and powerboat slips cannot be built in places manatees are commonly found. The Florida Marine Patrol helps to enforce these laws. A twenty-four-hour hot line lets people report any manatees that need help. Oceanarium staffs hurry to the rescue.

Public education programs have been sponsored by the Florida Power & Light Company. It commissions and distributes pamphlets, in English and Spanish, that tell boaters and divers how to avoid hurting manatees. The company also sponsors manatee research.

People working to save manatees point out that they help to clear aquatic weeds from bodies of water. This reduces the mosquito population and keeps waterways open. Both the United States and Mexico have tried clearing weed-clogged waterways by stocking them with manatees.

Gathering better information has been critical to helping manatees. A research center at Crystal River, Florida, has a Geographic Information System (GIS) with computerized maps that allows people to predict how changes in population, boat traffic, and other human activities might affect manatee habitats. People have charted the movements of manatees from the air to help develop protection zones where boat traffic can be controlled. From a Sea World blimp, antennas track manatees wearing radio collar tags.

The U.S. Fish and Wildlife Service uses radio and satellite telemetry to follow tagged manatees day and night, in changing weather conditions. They can even estimate the animal's speed. By understanding manatee habits, people can plan ways to manage human activities—such as boat speeds and routes—in order to protect the animals.

A CAPTIVE-BREEDING PROGRAM   Florida veterinarian Jesse R. White began working with manatees in 1969, when he helped to rescue a 1,000-pound (454-kilogram) manatee trapped in a storm drain in Fort Lauderdale. Later he developed a captive-breeding program at the Miami Seaquarium. Manatees were brought to the seaquarium in order to mate and give birth there. One manatee in the program gave birth to Lorelei, the first manatee ever produced in a captive, controlled setting. Seven more were born between 1975 and 1983.

White and his team worked hard to develop a feeding program for the manatees. Without the right balance of vitamins and minerals, the mothers might not bear young. The team grew aquatic food and served it with oats, wheat, apples, bananas, and carrots, along with calcium and phosphorus supplements.

Dr. White views his captive-breeding program as one way to save the manatee. Just twenty new captive-bred manatees might be enough to ensure the animal's continued existence. Captive animals can be carefully reintroduced to the wild and tracked with devices placed on their tails. By restocking waters with captive-bred manatees, and through public education, White believes future generations will be able to enjoy these appealing animals—animals many scientists call "the world's gentlest giant."

TWO

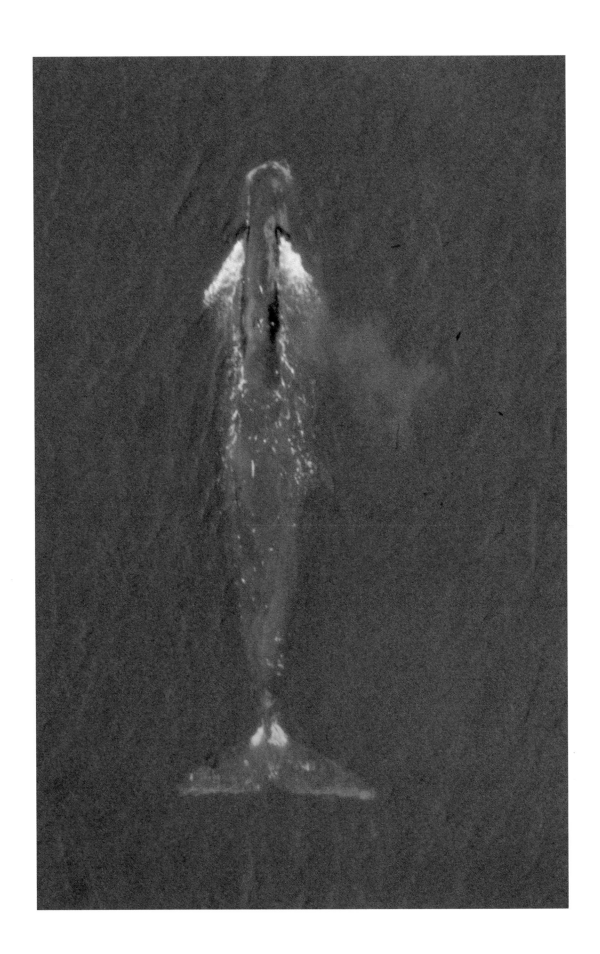

THE QUEST FOR A SAFE HABITAT

BOWHEAD WHALES

A whale surfacing on the water is an awesome sight. These huge, muscular creatures, with their massive heads and wide mouths, seem invincible. An old song calls the whale "a giant in might, where might is right, and King of the boundless sea." Yet eight species of whales now face extinction. They include the blue whale, which lives in all oceans. It can reach a length of 100 feet (30 meters) and weigh up to 220 tons (200 metric tons), the largest mammal that ever lived. In North America, the bowhead whale is endangered. It is also classified as endangered world-wide.

◆ ◆ ◆

Whales belong to the order Cetacea (from *cetus*, "whale" in Latin), along with porpoises and dolphins. Including about ninety-two kinds, whales make up the largest number of sea mammals. The two major groups of whales are the toothed whales (*odontocetes*), which have sharp teeth they use to catch fish or other marine mammals; and the baleen whales (*mysticetes*), whose toothless mouths contain rows of flexible plates called baleen rooted in the roof of the mouth. Baleen is made of keratin, the same material that is in human fingernails, and helps to strain seawater so baleen whales can feed on tiny plankton or other sea life.

The bowhead, a baleen whale, is known as *Balaena mysticetus* ("mustached whale" in Greek). It has about 700 baleen plates, each 10 feet (3 meters) long—the longest baleen of any whale. Both males and females are, on average, 50 feet (15 meters) long, with 65 feet (20 meters) being the maximum. They may weigh between 110 and 122 tons (99 to 110 metric tons).

Often females are larger than males. These whales can live to be more than thirty years of age.

Bowheads have smooth, velvety black skin with some gray near their tails, gray-toned flippers, and white or creamy chins. Some have black spots scattered on their necks and a thin white band near their tails. The calves are a pale blue-black color all over. They have a thicker, less sleek shape than mature whales.

COLD-WATER DIVERS

Throughout history, people have been fascinated by whales because of their fishlike form combined with a warm-blooded body that needs air to live. While fish have vertical tails and move from side to side when swimming, whales have horizontal tails and push themselves forward through the water. Their powerful tail muscles push upward to create a forward thrust; their fins steer and provide balance.

Bowheads are strong divers. They have reached depths of 5,000 feet (1,524 meters), although 3,500 feet (1,066 meters) is the norm. A bowhead usually stays underwater between ten and twenty minutes, but some have stayed submerged for up to an hour. Bowheads may rest on the surface of the water for half an hour at a time before submerging.

Whales are able to breathe through blowholes on their heads while continuing to swim forward. As a whale springs to the surface for air, its

Bowhead whales must come to the surface in order to breathe.

blowholes open and the characteristic spouting occurs, often with a rushing noise. The spray of air and water is called the "blow." A bowhead's blowholes are wide apart and send out two columns of spray that can spurt 23 feet (7 meters) high. This species has a nearly vertical dive and may surface more than once in about the same place.

Nearly hairless, bowheads have bristles on their heads and snouts. More body hair would slow them down. Blubber—a thick layer of fat beneath their skin—enables them to live in very cold water. They can maintain a body temperature of 99°F (37°C), close to that of humans, in near-freezing water.

There are four geographically separate populations of bowheads. In North America, they inhabit a region of drifting pack ice in the Arctic, between Greenland and Canada. They are the largest whales commonly found here. Bowheads favor bays and inlets but also venture into deeper waters. They are found in the Sea of Okhotsk; the Bering, Chukchi, and Beaufort Seas; the western Arctic (Baffin Bay and Davis Strait and their adjacent waters); and the Greenland and Barents Seas. Those in the last two seas are near extinction. A few hundred have been found around the Sea of Okhotsk and in the Baffin Bay and Davis Strait area.

Bowheads have been seen to pierce ice 3 inches (7.6 centimeters) thick in order to breathe, but they try to avoid frozen water. When fall arrives, they wait as long as possible and then return to their winter habitats. By September, ice has started to form in the northern part of their range as the water temperature dips below 30°F (-1°C). They then head south, where they can still break the surface easily enough to breathe. Some pass through the Bering Strait into the Bering Sea, moving into waters above the Aleutian and Kuril Islands. As the ice recedes in the spring, they move from the Bering Sea northeast into the Chukchi Sea, toward Banks and Prince Patrick Islands.

SOCIABLE AND INTELLIGENT   Scientists have found that whales have large, well-developed brains. Bowheads also have keen hearing but poor senses of smell and sight. Good eyesight is not much use in deep water, where hearing and the ability to sense vibrations provide more information. Whales also make sounds to which other whales respond. The bowheads' noises have been compared to thumps or taps.

Females vocalize to communicate with their calves, born in midwinter

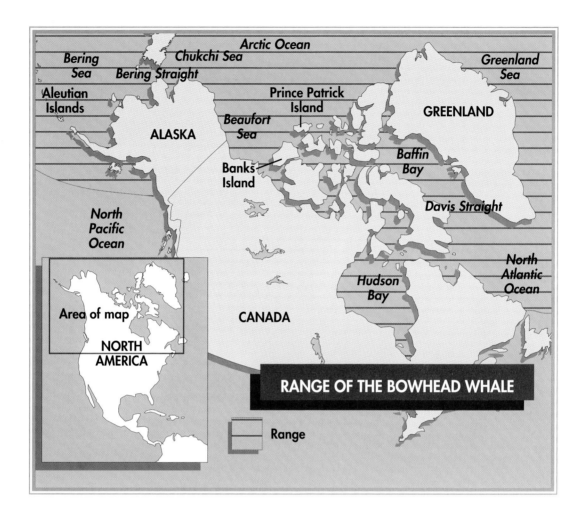

about ten to twelve months after mating. The calves are highly developed at birth, but they nurse for about a year until they reach 24 feet (7.3 meters) in length, twice their birth size. Females do not mate until they are between six and ten years of age, and they do not mate again for two to seven years after a birth.

Mother bowheads and their young live apart from the males. Mother–calf pairs and groups of six bowheads are commonly seen, and schools of up to fifty bowheads have been observed on rare occasions. Among other things, mother whales show their young where to find food.

Like seals and many other marine animals, bowheads eat plankton, microscopic plants and animals. This nourishing, basic food has been called "the pasture of the sea." Fringes along a bowhead's baleen plates trap plankton and small crustaceans such as krill and copepods that live in Arctic seas. After enough plankton collects on the baleen, the whale swallows, repeating this action as it eats vast amounts each day.

Mother bowheads and their calves travel in pairs and vocalize to communicate with each other.

Whales seek food both on the bottoms of shallow areas and on the surfaces of deeper water. Bowheads with their mouths coated with mud from the sea bottom have been seen in the Canadian Beaufort Sea. Groups may cooperate to catch food. Up to fourteen openmouthed bowheads have been spied swimming in a wedge-shaped pattern, forming a wall that prevents their prey from escaping.

A HUNTED ANIMAL   Whales have been hunted for thousands of years for their meat, blubber, and whalebone. The Inuit and other Arctic aboriginal peoples killed whales and used the whole animal for their basic needs. The large amount of meat fed many people.

As whale oil and baleen products gained popularity, whaling became big business. Blubber yielded oil for lamps, and "whalebone," as baleen was called, was used to make women's corsets and hoopskirts. During the 1700s, commercial whaling escalated. Black right whales, a relative of the bow-

This artist's rendition shows a bowhead's baleen, one of the things that made these animals so valuable to whalers.

head, were hunted vigorously. As their numbers declined, more bowheads were pursued. Once so numerous that whalers called it the "common whale" or *la baleine* ("the whale" in French), the bowhead was also named the great polar whale, arctic whale, and Greenland right whale until its bow-shaped skull led to the new, common name of "bowhead." Whalers hunted them off Greenland, and in Baffin and Hudson Bays. A commercial fishery opened in the Davis Strait during those years.

By the late 1700s, both bowheads and black right whales were gone from the North Atlantic. Seeking better hunting grounds, American whalers headed for the Sea of Okhotsk and the Bering Sea. Whalers often trapped a mother whale by harpooning her calf and dragging it off. The distressed mother would follow her baby toward shore, where the whaling crew could kill the mother more easily.

During the 1860s, the newly invented steamship and explosive harpoon gun enabled whalers to hunt whales faster and at less risk to themselves.

With the old methods, whales had had a chance to escape. Men chased them while riding in open whaleboats, aiming their hand-held harpoons at the physically superior animals. Under this new assault, the bowhead disappeared from the North Pacific, too.

By 1905, whalers were in the waters of Antarctica, the new center of the whaling industry. Factory ships were processing whale products faster than ever before. It is estimated that in 1938 alone, more than 46,000 whales were killed. The blue whale was almost extinct by the 1950s.

Plastic, flexible steel, and other inventions, however, made baleen far less valuable by the mid-1900s. Petroleum products and electricity had replaced whale oil. Still, there were whaling fleets all over the world in the early 1900s, and some whale ships exist today. Modern whalers can pursue groups of whales in remote places, locating them with helicopters. Exploding harpoons lead to an agonizing death. A grenade bursts inside the whale's stomach, after which it may suffer for an hour or longer before dying.

EFFORTS TO SAVE WHALES   A public outcry ensued after people became aware of the plight of whales and their potential extinction. Organizations such as Greenpeace promoted whale conservation, and some members attempted to stop the killing by placing themselves between the harpoon gun and the targeted whale. Their courage brought more public attention to the whales' plight. Photographs of whales being slaughtered appeared in newspapers, magazines, and on television programs. Scientists recorded "whale songs"—the melodious sounds made by bowhead, humpback, and black right whales—in order to present them as intelligent, feeling creatures. Statistics showed people that the numbers of many whale species were dwindling.

The United States and the United Kingdom were among the nations that stopped whaling in the 1960s, but other nations, including Japan and the former USSR, continued. The International Whaling Commission (IWC) set annual quotas—limits on the number of whales that could be killed. The IWC gave full protection to some whales, such as humpbacks, and gave limited protection to others.

In 1982, the IWC approved a complete ban on whaling. By 1986, it was illegal to hunt any whales for commercial purposes. At that time, the IWC estimated that there were only about 4,417 bowheads left. A 1978 survey of the Beaufort and Chukchi region had estimated that between

1,783 and 2,865 bowheads still lived there. There may have been as many as 36,000 bowheads in the Bering Sea before Yankee whalers arrived in the 1800s.

Some nations (Japan, Norway, and Iceland among them) later said they would not stop hunting whales. Since the 1986 ban took effect, more than 11,000 whales have been killed. The Japanese eat whale meat and claim that the minke whale population has recovered enough to be hunted in limited numbers. In 1992, some whaling nations had broken with the IWC and formed a separate group for those that continue the commercial hunting of whales.

DEALING WITH NEW THREATS   Today, few North Americans besides native peoples along the northern Alaska coast still hunt whales, but other things threaten their survival. Bowhead reproduction is slow, even under good conditions. Scientists fear the bowhead population has not increased at all since the 1970s, even though the whales are now protected. The few remaining bowheads live in a vast region and have trouble finding mates. Those who do meet may not be compatible or inclined to mate.

The fishing industry destroys some of the whales' food supply, or kills the whales by accident. Some become trapped in large fishing nets, along with turtles, sea lions, and dolphins. Water pollution is also a threat, as are noises that interfere with a whale's ability to navigate. Scientists have found that bowheads listen for subtle sounds in the water so they can determine the conditions of ice—whether it is moving and how deep or flat it might be. Ice conditions affect the way a whale's own voice echoes off the ice and the way that other whales sound when calling from a distance.

Another threat to bowheads is oil exploration in the Beaufort Sea, stretching from the North Slope of Alaska to northwestern Canada up to the Arctic Ocean. When oil-drilling plans were being made in the late 1970s, people wanted to predict the impact it would have on whales. In order to prepare the environmental impact statement that the government requires for such projects, an ecological research firm decided to study bowheads.

By measuring the whales' normal activities—the time they spend on the surface of the water and below, the duration of their dives, the number of blows they make with each surfacing—scientists would be able to judge what changes would occur as a result of human activity. For example, the scientists found that short, sudden changes in the bowheads' environment had significant effects. When a boat came by, for instance, the whales scattered, took shorter dives, and came up to breathe more often. Research on the bowhead continued into the 1980s. It was decided that when drilling began, no equipment that caused loud noises and strong vibrations in the water would be permitted within 5 miles (8 kilometers) of the whales.

But many conservationists argued that nobody had determined a truly safe distance for noises, nor did anyone know how drilling would affect whale migration patterns. They pointed out that the Endangered Species Act prohibits harassment of an endangered species—and couldn't drilling be viewed as harassment of the bowheads?

In the meantime, the World Wildlife Federation worked to define the boundaries of the bowheads' habitat between Greenland and Canada. During the 1990s, Inuit communities on Baffin Island were proposing an international biosphere reserve that would include the whales' critical habitat. Concerned individuals joined groups that hoped to save whales. They wrote letters to legislators and took part in boycotts of products from whaling nations. These efforts show a desire to protect the seas, which cover most of the earth, and their inhabitants. Whales, once looked upon as a product at people's disposal, are now seen as having the right to continued existence on this planet.

THREE

Stranded on Tall Peaks

MOUNT GRAHAM RED SQUIRRELS

Red squirrels are a common sight in wooded rural and suburban areas throughout the continental United States, Alaska, and Canada. Despite the disappearance of millions of acres of the woodlands they once inhabited, most types of squirrels have managed to thrive. Yet a few of these seed-loving rodents are now dangerously rare. The Mount Graham red squirrel of the Pinaleno Mountains of Graham County in southeast Arizona is at risk.

The squirrels occupy Mount Graham and Webb, Hawk, High, Emerald, and Heliograph Peaks in the Pinalenos. Scientists first collected these small mammals from the mountains in 1894.

By 1965, this mammal was thought to be extinct. A few years later, some squirrels were found, and today there may be only about 200 of these small survivors. The squirrel is on the Arizona Game and Fish Department's list of threatened native wildlife in Arizona and is classified as "endangered" by the federal government.

◆ ◆ ◆

Like other squirrels, the Mount Graham type (*Tamiasciurus hudsonicus grahamensis*) belongs to the order Rodentia, which includes mice, skunks, hamsters, beavers, and porcupines. In common with all rodents, the squirrel has four long, chisellike teeth built for gnawing the plant foods that make up its diet.

The Mount Graham squirrel is tiny, weighing a mere 8 ounces (224 grams) and measuring about 8 inches (20 centimeters) in length, with a 6-inch- (15-centimeter-) long, fluffy tail. Unlike many other squirrels, the Mount Graham species does not have a white-fringed tail. Females and males look much alike; they are grayish brown in color and have rusty and yellowish markings along their backs. Their underfur is white, with a dark line running through it during the summer.

Coniferous, or cone-bearing, trees, abundant on the Pinalenos, are used by the squirrel for both housing and food. The squirrels build their nests in tree cavities or in crotches against the trunks. They eat the seeds of pine, fir, and spruce cones, along with mushrooms, fungi, and other plants. When danger, in the form of a raptor or weasel, appears, the squirrels seek refuge in tree cavities.

Observers have noted that the squirrels mate and become pregnant in the spring or early summer. Babies are born from late spring to late summer. Females may produce one to two litters a year, with three to four young in each litter.

A distinguishing feature of these squirrels is that they do not chatter like other squirrels. The Mount Graham squirrel is silent except when facing danger. At those times, it makes an unusual explosive, ratchetlike call that has been described as a *chr-r-RR-RR* sound. Scientists think that because these squirrels have lived apart from most other squirrels for thousands of years, they had less need to vocalize.

Active year-round, the squirrels are awake in the daytime and sometimes on moonlit nights. During a heavy storm, the squirrels may retreat to their nests. In the wintertime, they make tunnels under the snow to reach their food supply.

AN UNUSUAL HABITAT

Rising above the desert of southeast Arizona, Mount Graham is 10,720 feet (3,267 meters) high. It is what scientists call a "biologically unique area," for on its peaks live eighteen species and subspecies of plants and animals that exist nowhere else on earth. A spruce-fir forest at the summit is the home of the Mount Graham red squir-

Trees provide Mount Graham squirrels with food and a place to build their nests.

rel. Other animals sharing this lofty habitat are the Mexican spotted owl and the Apache trout, both considered to be threatened with extinction. The Pinaleno pocket gopher, long-tailed vole, and northern goshawk are considered to be vulnerable to extinction, though not yet threatened.

Some 11,000 years ago, at the end of the most recent ice age, the Pinaleno Mountains became separated from other mountains in the region. As sheets of ice moved northward, the steep peaks were left isolated, with spruce-fir forests growing on their tops. Below, a desert, later called the Sonoran Desert, took shape.

Those insects, birds, reptiles, and mammals that could not survive in the dry desert heat found a home on the mountain peaks. They were an unusual assortment, made up of animals that had originated from the north and those that had come from Mexico. Among these was the species of red squirrel now called the Mount Graham. The red squirrels became adapted to life on the mountain. The thick canopy of spruce and corkbark fir trees and old growth forest on the mountain provided the humidity and other conditions they needed to survive.

The squirrels have their own important role in the ecosystem. Their use of cones helps with the planting and sprouting of seeds throughout the forest. They may also scatter fungi throughout the forest as they eat por-

◆ MIDDENS FOR SURVIVAL ◆

In its ongoing search for seeds, the Mount Graham squirrel competes with the birds and chipmunks that share the forest. Spruce cones containing seeds are most abundant in late summer, so that is when the squirrels collect cones for the winter. Thousands of cones become part of what is called a midden. Each squirrel builds its own midden in a damp area of thick woods, a hollow log, or a stump that is away from the sunlight. Dampness prevents the cones from opening before the seeds are needed.

A biologist from the Arizona Game and Fish Department measures the temperature of a midden.

To construct a midden, the squirrel sits on a branch eating the seeds from a cone, then drops the leftovers on the ground. Deep layers build up. To those layers, the squirrel adds fresh cones. Eventually, the midden grows to include piles of cones, scales, mushrooms, cored cones, and other things. The midden may be 12 or more feet (3.6 or more meters) across and more than 1 foot (30 centimeters) deep. Upon examining middens, scientists have found a variety of cones—Douglas fir, Englemann spruce, corkbark fir, white fir, and white pine.

During winter when snow covers the midden, a squirrel has to tunnel its way to reach the stored food. As one might guess, the squirrels are quite possessive of their middens and show their wrath toward any other animal that comes near.

tions of those plants and excrete spores that they cannot digest. As the spores make contact with tree roots, they germinate and grow.

CHALLENGES TO SURVIVAL   For centuries, the red squirrels lived quietly along the mountain slopes. At one time, they made their homes as far down as 6,500 feet (1,981 meters) above sea level. Occasionally, hunters killed some squirrels. Some trees were cut down, starting in the 1800s. Then, in the 1930s, loggers began vigorously harvesting the rich forests in the mountains, which included oak, ponderosa pine, and Douglas fir on the lower slopes.

Logging pushed the red squirrel higher up the mountain. During the 1940s, a new threat arrived. The tufted-eared, or Abert, squirrel was brought into the lower areas of the mountain to live and breed for the benefit of hunters. As their habitats became more crowded, the Mount Graham squirrels relocated even higher up the mountain.

As the squirrels worked to adjust to a shrinking habitat, some continued to die from naturally occurring problems—seasonal droughts, lightning fires, and a lack of food. Squirrels can also die from viral illnesses and a disease called tularemia, but scientists are not sure which diseases are present among the Mount Graham population. Although predators of the squirrel include the black bear, coyote, bobcat, peregrine falcon, red-tailed hawk, spotted owl, great horned owl, and reptiles such as rattlesnakes and the gopher snake, the Arizona Game and Fish Department has found that few red squirrels are killed by predators.

Thus the worst threat to the squirrels remains the destruction of their habitats, which deprives them of nesting places and food. When the trees have been cut from an area, the squirrels leave. As fewer squirrels inhabit smaller, more isolated areas, reproduction becomes a problem, as it is for the manatee, bowhead whale, and Florida panther. A reduced choice of mates means less genetic diversity. The traits in a shrinking gene pool may not be broad enough to produce hardy offspring.

SAVING THE MOUNT GRAHAM SQUIRREL
During the 1980s, it became clear that the Mount Graham squirrel was in danger. Only a few squirrels were being seen each year. Squirrel hunting on the mountain was therefore banned. The area in which Mount Graham is found, now called the Coronado National Forest, was designated as protected federal land.

Conservationists urged that the old growth conditions of the land be restored and that no logging be permitted on the land above 9,000 feet (2,743 meters), where the squirrels now live. They also advocated that an area be set aside for wildlife and that no roads, campers, or human activity be permitted there.

One long-term plan will allow more trees in the Coronado National Forest to grow to maturity. The Arizona Game and Fish Department has

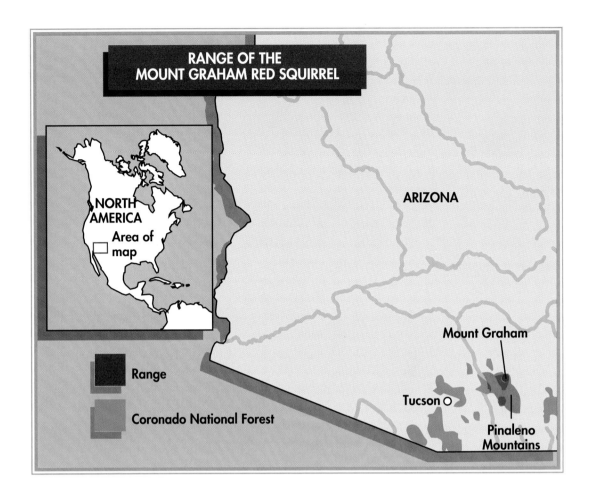

RANGE OF THE
MOUNT GRAHAM RED SQUIRREL

NORTH AMERICA
Area of map

ARIZONA

Mount Graham

Tucson ○

Pinaleno Mountains

■ Range

■ Coronado National Forest

recommended that no timber be harvested on slopes from the northwest to the east to allow more stands of spruce-firs, Douglas firs, and white firs. An increase in the number of cone-bearing trees should also help the squirrels to survive.

As these plans take shape, the squirrels are being studied to determine their actual population and to find out if they return to forests that have been allowed to renew themselves. Scientists are also trying to determine what effect other kinds of squirrels have on the Mount Graham type.

A NEW THREAT   With high elevation and clear overhead skies, the Mount Graham area has been called a perfect place for stargazing. In the early 1980s, the University of Arizona proposed building a $200-million astronomical facility on Emerald Peak. The university planned to set up seven telescopes on an area of about 7 to 8 acres (2.8 to 3.2 hectares). Eventually, there would be eighteen telescopes on peaks and knolls over a

Biologists worked together to take a survey of the squirrel population on Mount Graham.

3,500-acre (1,400-hectare) area that would include most of the land above 9,400 feet (2,865 meters) on Mount Graham and the other Pinaleno peaks. Supporting facilities would also be built: a dormitory, workshops, garages, and a visitor center.

A controversy immediately erupted over the proposed Mount Graham International Observatory. Opponents, including biologists and botanists, said the observatory would destroy the animals and plants in this critical habitat, particularly those on the summit. At least 113 of the remaining Mount Graham squirrels live in this area. Some organizations that had planned to be part of the telescope project (the Smithsonian Institution, Ohio State University, and the University of Chicago) withdrew, citing environmental reasons.

The University of Arizona and its partners, Germany's Max Planck Institute, the Arcetri Observatory of Italy, and the Tucson-based Research Corporation, say that an observatory can co-exist with wildlife. Officials from these groups claim that scientific research conducted from this site would help us to understand more about the origins of the universe. The university says that this area has already been logged and is used by people (Bible classes, for example) every summer. Some also say that Mount Graham squirrels may not be crucial in any way to our planet.

In the late 1980s, the observatory project went forward despite objections. Two telescopes were set up in the Pinalenos, and a third site was selected in the forest near Emerald Peak. In 1988, some of the university's proposals were reviewed by the National Park Service, which denied some and approved others with restrictions. But then Congress passed a controversial act that exempted the three telescopes from the National Environmental Policy Act and the Endangered Species Act. A telescope called the Columbus, the largest so far, was slated to be put up about a half mile (0.8 kilometer) from the site that had been selected on Emerald Peak. With it would come a new road through the northernmost forest, segmenting it still further.

The university said that building on this new site would pose less harm

This is one of the telescopes under construction at the Mount Graham International Observatory.

to the squirrels than the original Emerald Peak site, but opponents point out that other living things are also at risk. The new site has the highest plant diversity in the Pinalenos. Also, any telescope located on this exposed peak could be seen from a distance, possibly frightening animals away.

During the early 1990s, opponents to the project formed a group called the Mount Graham Coalition and continued to protest bitterly. They claimed that Congress had based its ruling on false information about the survival prospects of the Mount Graham squirrel and asked the Forest Service to review the situation. The coalition, which included local Audubon chapters, with support from the National Wildlife Federation, Sierra Club, and some University of Arizona students, hoped for legislation that would halt the new telescope and require that another study be done before any more habitat was destroyed. They also asked that the existing telescopes be removed. To support their case, they claimed that the Hubble Space Telescope, launched from a space shuttle, makes such earth-based astronomy projects obsolete and unnecessary.

Local Native Americans have also protested the observatory. The San Carlos Apaches consider Mount Graham a sacred site in their religion—the home of the mountain spirits who taught their tribe to hunt. They claim the observatory violates the Native American Religious Freedom Act of 1968 and the National Historic Preservation Act. In 1992, a court ruled in favor of the University of Arizona, but the Apaches have appealed that decision.

The debate over the Mount Graham Observatory shows how broad-ranging and divisive environmental issues can be. Some organizations, such as the Smithsonian Institution, have long supported both environmental concerns and astronomy. They support Native American interests, too. One issue at the heart of the matter is whether more knowledge about the stars and other astronomical subjects is worth the potential loss of animal and plant species and unique natural settings. To those who say it is not, the answer is to avoid tampering with the peaks of Mount Graham and allow the squirrels and other living things to exist as they did years ago.

Terry B. Johnson of the Arizona Game and Fish Department has said that management of Mount Graham "must preclude anything that negatively impacts spruce-corkbark-fir forest and middens or impedes their development. . . . If we protect the ecosystem, the individual species will also be protected."

LESSER LONG-NOSED BAT

FOUR

Nighttime Helpers

LONG-NOSED BATS

When thinking about bats, many people shudder. Bats are viewed as strange and menacing creatures that swoop about in the nighttime, sucking blood and carrying diseases. Through the years, millions of bats have been killed by people who feared or disliked them.

But bats play an important role in nature. There are between 1,000 and 2,000 different species of bats—the largest number of species of any mammal. Bats eat vast numbers of insect pests, such as mosquitoes; pollinate many important plants; and spread seeds. Up to 95 percent of the seed spreading needed for forest regrowth in tropical rain forests, which are vital to human survival, is done by bats. They eat fruits, then expel the seeds as they fly over the forest, thus "planting" more trees and shrubs.

Some species of bats are already extinct, and others are threatened, the result of pollution, habitat destruction, and killings by humans. In North America, 40 percent of all bat species are threatened or endangered. The long-nosed bats (genus: *Leptonycteris*) that live in the southwestern United States and Mexico joined the endangered list during the late 1980s. If they die, a number of plants and other animals might disappear with them.

NIGHT-FLYING MAMMALS   Bats, the only mammals that fly, come in many sizes, with an array of fascinating features. Some, like the fruit-eating bats of the Old World tropics, have a wingspan of nearly 6 feet (1.8 meters), while the bumblebee bat, an insect-eating bat of Thailand (the tiniest mammal on earth), weighs about as much as a grape.

41 ◆

Long-nosed bats are medium-sized, usually weighing about ½ to 1 ounce (14 to 28 grams). The Goodman's long-nosed bat that lives in western Mexico is about 20 to 22 inches (51 to 56 centimeters) long and weighs about ¼ ounce (7 grams). It is a dark color. The Mexican long-nosed bat, which lives in New Mexico, Texas, and Mexico, has a wingspan of about 22 to 28 inches (56 to 71 centimeters). It is a dark brown color on its back and a lighter brown on its stomach. Some males are more reddish brown in color. Similar in appearance is the Sanborn's long-nosed bat (also called the lesser long-nosed bat), which lives in dry parts of northern Mexico and, in summer, southern Arizona.

Although bats are not blind, as some people think, they rely on a system called echolocation to get around at night, rather than sight. Using their amazing sonar (sound-sensing) ability, bats emit loud, high-frequency bursts of sound that bounce off the objects around them. Through sound, bats sense where things are so they can avoid obstacles and head toward desired objects, such as mosquitoes or plants. The unusually long ears on some kinds of bats help them to do this.

Bats are skilled navigators. Dr. Merlin D. Tuttle, an expert on bats, has said, "With extreme precision, bats can perceive motion, distance, speed, trajectory, and shape. They can detect and avoid obstacles no thicker than a human hair."

Long-nosed bats use some echolocation to get around. But scientists think that their small ears may be evidence that they depend more on their sense of smell to find the plants whose nectar and fruits they eat.

Bats can be found in most parts of the world except in the polar regions, where the climate is too cold. Shy and fearful of humans, they make their homes in caves, abandoned mines, and tree cavities. Bats in cold climates hibernate during the winter, staying inactive and living off the fat stores in their bodies.

Long-nosed bats live in the desert, primarily

LESSER LONG-NOSED BAT
Leptonycteris curasoae
- KINGDOM: Animalia
- PHYLUM: Chordata
- CLASS: Mammalia
- ORDER: Chiroptera
- FAMILY: Phyllostomidae
- GENUS: *Leptonycteris*
- SPECIES: *curasoae*

MEXICAN LONG-NOSED BAT
Leptonycteris nivalis
- KINGDOM: Animalia
- PHYLUM: Chordata
- CLASS: Mammalia
- ORDER: Chiroptera
- FAMILY: Phyllostomidae
- GENUS: *Leptonycteris*
- SPECIES: *nivalis*

MEXICAN LONG-NOSED BAT

in the Sonoran Desert of the southwestern United States and Mexico. They inhabit caves most of the time and roost in groups ranging from a few bats to several thousand. Like other bats, during the breeding season, long-nosed females join special nursery colonies where they raise their young. Scientists think they mate and bear young during the summer.

Long-nosed bats are among those that eat plants for food. Other bat species prefer fish, frogs, rats, and many kinds of insects, including pests that destroy crops and spread diseases. The little brown bat, one of the most common species in America, can eat 600 mosquitoes in just an hour!

POLLINATING THE LAND   Long-nosed bats are plant eaters that suck the nectar from different kinds of century plants (Mexican agaves), giant cacti (saguaros), and organ-pipe cacti. Long snouts and long, stretching tongues enable long-nosed bats to reach plant nectar. Their tongues move easily in and out of their mouths; the brushlike tips of their tongues help them to move pollen and nectar inside.

When long-nosed bats leave a flower, their faces and fur are coated

Long-nosed bats often gather in caves in groups.

with pollen, which they transfer to the next plant while feeding. This process of bringing male pollen to the female flower is needed if the plants are to reproduce. After feeding, the bats return to their roosts to groom the pollen off their faces and sleep while they digest their food.

Bats migrating from Mexico each spring follow a trail of blooming cacti northward through the Sonoran Desert. The flowers of the saguaro cacti, one of the foods for these bats, begin to bloom in early spring. These cacti stand from 5 feet (1.5 meters) to almost 23 feet (7 meters) tall, and the bats flit among them. Besides pollinating the plants, the bats eat their fruits, then spread the seeds around as they excrete them while flying over the desert.

Long-nosed bats and other animals that pollinate vital plants are called "keystone species." This means that they sustain plants that other animals need for food and shelter. A great many animals, including bees, moths, finches, hummingbirds, sparrows, orioles, field mice, and lizards, depend on the plants pollinated by long-nosed bats. Because the petals of most of these plants open chiefly at night, bats are their main pollinators. It has been found that bats are better at pollinating agave plants than either bees or doves are. Scientists who studied agave pollination found that thousands more new plant seeds developed in areas with bats than in areas without them. This system of pollination serves both bats and plants well.

These plants are important cash crops for the people in the regions where they grow. The agave plant is the source of the liquid used to make a liquor called tequila. Producing tequila is a large industry in Mexico. Some species of agave have also been used since ancient times for their fiber, called henequen, which is still an important source of export income. It is important to preserve wild strains of these plants in their natural settings so that genetic material will be available for the future growth of agave plants. The loss of long-nosed bats threatens the survival of these plants. Yet, until recently, many people regarded bats as nuisances and did not realize their value in ecosystems.

BATS UNDER SIEGE   People who have tried to rescue the world's bats say that bats have a serious public relations problem. Through the centuries, myths about bats have made them unpopular with most people. They have been associated with vampires, and people fear that they suck human or animal blood. There are only three species of vampire bats that live on animal blood, and each is about the size of a mouse and lives only in Central

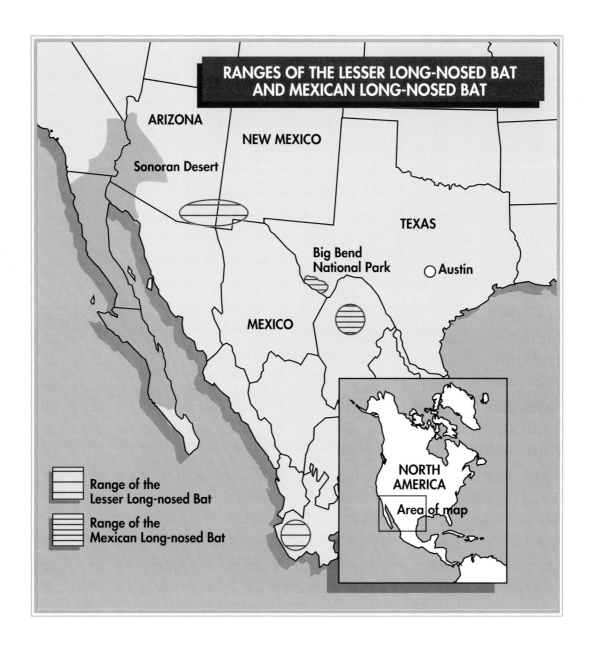

RANGES OF THE LESSER LONG-NOSED BAT
AND MEXICAN LONG-NOSED BAT

ARIZONA

NEW MEXICO

Sonoran Desert

TEXAS

Big Bend
National Park   ○ Austin

MEXICO

Range of the
Lesser Long-nosed Bat

Range of the
Mexican Long-nosed Bat

NORTH
AMERICA

Area of map

and South America. Nor do bats fly into people's hair or seek human contact. Only sick bats approach humans.

It has long been feared that bats spread rabies (a fatal disease of the central nervous system that causes animals to behave in an unnatural, disoriented way) and other diseases. In the 1960s, there were rumors that bats could carry rabies without showing the symptoms. These rumors were later shown to be false. Says bat expert Merlin Tuttle, "Bats can get rabies, the same as dogs and cats can, but when they do get it they die quickly, just as other animals do. Anyway, less than half of 1 percent of bats contract rabies, and, unlike most mammals, even when bats are rabid they rarely become aggressive."

Still, many people kill bats in their home attics or barns, often with a poison called chlorophacinone (Rozol), which has uncertain effects on human health. People also shoot bats in caves. Eagle Creek Cave in Arizona once held the largest known colony of Mexican free-tailed bats. The huge colony ate about 350,000 pounds (158,757 kilograms) of insects each night. By 1969, 99.9 percent (some thirty million bats) had disappeared. Shotgun-shell casings littered the cave entrance. This has happened in numerous caves throughout the world. Bats are easy to kill because they roost close together in large groups. Although some live thirty years, a fairly long life for a mammal, they produce only one pup a year.

Bat populations die out for other reasons. In Asia and on Pacific islands, they are killed for food. Cave exploration leads to deaths. If people intrude, mothers may move their offspring to parts of the cave where it is not warm enough for a pup to survive. After the Colossal Cave in New Mexico was opened to tourists in the 1950s, all 20,000 of the Sanborn's long-nosed bats that lived there died. The loss of their habitats or the destruction of their food plants can be devastating to bats.

Hibernating bats die when disturbed, too. During the winter, they don't eat but use their body fat to survive. When a bat is disturbed, its body temperature will rise sharply as it gets ready to flee. When this happens repeatedly, the bat uses up so much energy that its supply of body fat is depleted and it dies of starvation.

During the 1980s, scientists found that the populations of long-nosed bats were declining throughout their range. The summer bat population of Big Bend National Park in Texas was much lower. Various caves in Arizona held fewer bats or were empty. No colonies of Mexican long-nosed bats could be found in central Mexico. By 1987, both the Mexican long-nosed bat and Sanborn's long-nosed bat were added to the U.S. Fish and Wildlife Service's list of endangered species.

Scientists viewed habitat destruction as the major reason for the bats' decline. A less frequent hazard was cattlemen who accidentally killed long-nosed bats instead of cattle-biting vampire bats who often share the same caves. Loss of plants they need for food along their migratory paths accounted for other casualties. People who want to make their own tequila take plants from the desert where bats regularly come for food. In 1988, in an area of the Sonoran Desert in northwestern Mexico bordering the Gulf of California, scientists found only a few hundred bats eating at night where twenty years ago there were thousands.

SAVING THE BATS For many years, bats were neglected by conservationists. During the 1980s, some people set out to change this but were told that nobody was interested in bats. Spurred by scientist and photographer Merlin Tuttle, a small group formed Bat Conservation International (BCI), devoted to the study and conservation of bats. The organization has its headquarters in Austin, Texas, a state with thirty-two species of bats, the largest number in the United States.

Tuttle has photographed more than 300 kinds of bats around the world and found innovative ways to catch and release them unharmed. He points out that bats are usually so frightened when approached to be photographed that they snarl and bare their teeth in self-defense. Tuttle's sensitive handling of these bats results in photos of appealing animals that display intelligence, curiosity, and feeling. He shows the photographs all over the world as he discusses the importance of bats.

Bat Conservation International has taught many people why bats are valuable to ecosystems. Their pamphlet, "Why Save Bats?" has been widely distributed. It has helped to raise money and increase membership for BCI, which had more than 10,000 members in over fifty-five countries by 1990. BCI shows people who do not want bats around how to get them out of their homes without using poison. The organization has taught people in the tropics how to get rid of troublesome vampire bats without killing helpful long-nosed bats.

Another effort has been directed toward farmers who fear bats will eat their crops. In recent years, the Israeli government poisoned large numbers of fruit bats, and Israel's insect population soared as a result. When a pest's natural enemies are destroyed, more chemical pesticides are usually needed—something that can harm the environment. It has been shown that bats eat only very ripe fruit, and usually, growers harvest it before then. By eating fruit-fly larvae, moth caterpillars, and root worms, bats can help farmers.

In 1989, Bat Conservation International began a multiyear project to study long-nosed bats in the Sonoran Desert of Arizona and Mexico. A grant from the National Geographic Society allowed scientists to study the relationship between these bats and the organ-pipe, saguaro, and cardon

◆ A REAL-LIFE "BATMAN" ◆

Merlin Tuttle has long been fascinated by living things. His father, a biology teacher, kept reptiles and amphibians as pets. As a child, Tuttle reared monarch butterflies and studied small mammals, such as shrews. In the summer he helped raise birds and animals that his father used in teaching nature classes at Yosemite National Park.

Merlin D. Tuttle

When Tuttle was sixteen, his family moved to Tennessee, not far from a bat cave, and he began studying them. Two years later, he met with experts at the Smithsonian Institution to discuss bats. In college, he majored in mammalogy—the study of mammals—and visited Venezuela's rain forest to learn about the mammals that live there. He also made hundreds of trips to bat caves around North America.

After college, Dr. Tuttle became a museum curator and is today a respected scientist. He continues to study bats around the world. One day in 1976, he was shocked to find that a colony of some 250,000 bats that had lived in Hambrick Cave in Alabama had been killed with sticks, stones, and guns. He decided to educate the public and to begin an organization to save bats.

In 1982, Dr. Tuttle and some other conservationists formed Bat Conservation International (BCI). Bats were then seen as an unpopular cause. Tuttle's books, articles, speeches, and photographs of bats helped people to see them as worthwhile creatures. BCI has changed people's attitudes and has saved bat colonies around the world.

One of Tuttle's achievements was persuading the owners of Hambrick Cave—the Tennessee Valley Authority (TVA)—to protect any bats that returned there. After a fence was built to keep people out, bats reestablished a colony at the cave.

Tuttle claims that people need not fear bats. In 1990, he said, "Just leave bats alone and the odds of being harmed are infinitesimally small. Only about fifteen people in the whole of the United States and Canada are believed to have died of *any* bat-related disease in the past four decades. . . . When people *are* endangered, it's usually because they've foolishly picked up a sick bat that bites in self-defense."

Bats around the Congress Avenue Bridge, once viewed as a nuisance, have now become a tourist attraction.

cacti. Such studies teach people what is at stake if long-nosed bats decline, and they show scientists how to help bats survive in their habitats.

Other bat conservation projects have been successful, too. In 1990, people in Austin, Texas, wanted to get rid of a large colony of bats that had settled in the remodeled Congress Avenue Bridge. Nearly a million of them migrated to that spot each summer. BCI members explained that bats were no threat and would eat many insects—some 15,000 to 30,000 pounds (6,803 to 13,607 kilograms) each night. People began to see them as valuable and to watch them with interest. The city even erected an educational exhibit at the bridge.

Merlin Tuttle heard that some land in Florida that included a cave housing thousands of gray and other species of bats was about to be sold. The buyer planned to turn the land into a housing development. Tuttle spoke with the developer and invited the man and his family to see some bats and watch the colony flying at night. After that, the developer decided to sell the land with the cave intact, at a loss, to The Nature Conservancy, a nonprofit organization devoted to preserving important habitats. The state of Florida now protects the cave.

Since scientists now realize that bats may die when disturbed during hibernation and pup-rearing times, they avoid entering caves at those times to band the bats with identification tags. Members of the National Speleological Society, a group of experienced cave explorers, have developed ways to enter caves without harming bats. But amateurs may not be so careful.

Young people are also helping to save endangered bats. One of them, Bert Grantges, became interested in bats when he was four years old. By age ten, he was already giving lectures on bats to conservation groups; by the time he was in high school, he had become a spokesperson for Bat Conservation International.

Around the country, people have helped bats by setting up bat houses in their yards. These floorless wooden houses shelter bats, who reward their hosts by eating mosquitoes and other pests.

In December 1992, the First Latin American Mammal Congress was held. More than a hundred people from thirteen countries heard from animal researchers, including a representative from BCI. One day of the week-long event was devoted to bats and bat conservation in Latin America. The risks to long-nosed bats living in that part of the world were discussed, along with long-range plans to save them through international cooperation.

Merlin Tuttle says, "It's an unfortunate reality that by and large the high proportion of conservation efforts around the world have involved the cute and cuddly and glamorous. But the cuteness of an animal is in no way a measure of its ecological or economic value."

GRAY WOLF

FIVE

Hunted to Death

The GRAY WOLF AND THE RED WOLF

For centuries, people have viewed wolves as their enemies. Hearing their nighttime howls and seeing wolf tracks near the bony remains of dead animals, people thought wolves would attack them and their livestock. The Europeans who settled in North America saw wolves as a threat and also as their rivals in hunting deer and other game the settlers used for food. For those reasons, they killed wolves by the millions.

In recent decades, scientists have learned a great deal about wolves. Many now think that these intelligent, sociable creatures rarely approach humans—and then almost always in a harmless way. Since the 1970s, concerned people have worked to save America's endangered red and gray wolves.

FRIENDLY PACK ANIMALS Wolves belong to the order of mammals called Carnivora (from the Latin *carnivorous*, meaning meat eaters) and are the largest members of the Canidae family, which includes dogs, jackals, and foxes. Adult wolves weigh between 40 and 175 pounds (18 and 79 kilograms) and measure about 6 feet (1.8 meters) from their noses to the tips of their tails.

More than 10,000 years ago, the breeds of dogs that became the pets of today were domesticated, or tamed to live among humans. Although wolves remained wild animals, they still have many traits in common with dogs. They are intelligent and will befriend people whom they know well. Wolves like to communicate, and they show affection through noises, nuzzling, licking, touching, and wagging their tails. They take good care of their pups and are loyal to their families and other members of their packs (groups of wolves that live together).

Wolf packs are well organized, and members cooperate to survive. Packs may include from two to thirty-six wolves, but the usual number is between five and eight. This includes a male leader and his mate, along with their young and some of their relatives. Together, the group travels, hunts, shares food, and raises pups.

The pack leader is not always the strongest or the largest male in the group. Experience, personality, and communication skills count for more than size. The leader decides where and how the group will hunt, and he settles fights among members. His mate, the head female, seems to lead other females, young wolves, and sometimes weak males. When leaders become too old, younger ones take over.

Wolves mate at age two or three and may stay with their mates for life. If the food supply is low, only the male and female pack leaders may have pups. New pups are born in the spring. To get ready, the female, alone or with her mate, digs a new den in a hillside, under a fallen tree, or at the base

Gray wolf pups stay with their mother until the age of two.

of a large tree. She may also use an abandoned beaver lodge, a fox den, or a rock cave. When the litter, usually six pups, is born, the mother stays with them in her den while other pack members seek food.

The whole pack plays with the pups and guards them against enemies, such as bears. By the age of three or four weeks, wolf pups are eating meat along with their mother's milk. Soon they venture outside to play. They practice hunting by pouncing on each other's tails and on insects and small animals. By autumn, they are hunting with the adults but do not help with the kill. At the age of two, some wolves leave the group to find mates and to start new packs. Usually half the pups in a litter reach adulthood. The others die from disease, parasites, fire, starvation, or are killed by predators, including humans.

SURVIVING IN DIFFERENT REGIONS
Wolves once lived everywhere in the world except Antarctica, Africa, and Australia. Some two million wolves lived throughout North America from coast to coast and from Canada to Mexico. They can survive in many climates and in such diverse places as pine forests, mountains, prairies, swamps, grasslands, and even the barren Arctic tundra, where temperatures can dip to -50°F (-46°C).

Wolves in colder climates have shaggy coats, nearly 3 inches (8 centimeters) thick, that repel water. They stay warm by sleeping in a curled-up position with their noses tucked beneath their bushy tails. In the summer, a similar position helps them to keep insects away from their faces and eyes. Webbed paws allow wolves to walk across slippery ice. These widened paws also make good swimming paddles in warmer weather. Wolves may swim when pursuing a beaver or caribou, but those animals usually outswim them.

Wherever they live, wolves eat mostly meat. Those in warmer climates add a bit of fruit. They eat lizards, ducks, fish, birds, and small mammals. But their mainstay is mammals larger than themselves—caribou, deer, elk, bighorn sheep, and moose. They look for stragglers in a herd and kill the sick, injured, or very old.

Except in the rare case of a wolf who lives alone, hunting is a group task. Wolves move at speeds of 5 to 45 miles (8 to 72 kilometers) per hour and may travel 40 miles (64 kilometers) at a stretch in search of food. The game they hunt tower over them and can weigh more than 1,000 pounds (464 kilograms). Moose are so strong and fast that about 90 percent of them

Gray wolves usually hunt in groups, in order to bring down large prey.

escape. To catch such animals, wolves form a circle and attack from different sides with their sharp, pointed teeth. After a kill, each wolf, starting with the pack leader, eats 10 to 20 pounds (4.5 to 9 kilograms) of meat. Wolves share food, especially with pack members too old or weak to hunt. When prey is scarce, they may go for two weeks or more without eating.

By killing game, wolves play a key role in their ecosystems. When herds become too large, many animals starve, or they overgraze, crowding out smaller animals. In places where wolves have died out, elk multiplied and crowded out beaver. Without beavers, rangeland can dry out, resulting in more fires.

Gray Wolf (Timber Wolf)
Canis lupus

> **KINGDOM:** Animalia
> **PHYLUM:** Chordata
> **CLASS:** Mammalia
> **ORDER:** Carnivora
> **FAMILY:** Canidae
> **GENUS:** *Canis*
> **SPECIES:** *lupus*

THE DISAPPEARING GRAY WOLF

Two types of wolves—the gray wolf (*Canis lupus*) and red wolf (*Canis rufus*)—still live in North America. Of the twenty-four kinds of gray wolves, eight appear to be extinct. Two of the three types of red wolves also seem to be extinct. One species that has disappeared from the wild is the Great Plains (buffalo) gray wolf. A few Great Plains wolves still live in captivity in the state of

Washington. Many of the gray wolves now in America are known as timber wolves. Their coats are shades of gray, brown, and beige with black markings on their tops, sides, and backs. They stand about 26 to 38 inches (66 to 97 centimeters) high and weigh 60 to 157 pounds (27 to 71 kilograms).

Some 5,900 to 7,200 gray wolves live in Alaska and thousands more live in Canada, but few remain in the continental United States. In 1991, the U.S. Fish and Wildlife Service estimated that there were 1,600 wolves in Minnesota, 20 on Isle Royale in Lake Superior, 40 in Wisconsin, 50 in Montana, and perhaps 15 in Idaho. Endangered in every state but Alaska and Minnesota (where they are considered threatened), wolves occupy only 1 percent of their former range. Some died out when their habitats and food were severely reduced, but most died at the hands of humans.

During the 1800s and early 1900s, American settlers trapped, poisoned, shot, clubbed, and strangled wolves. As settlers killed much of the large game wolves hunted for food, wolf packs resorted to killing the settlers' cows and sheep. The U.S. government supported farmers and ranchers in their efforts to kill wolves, which included setting out poisoned meat. The poisoned meat not only killed the wolves but also killed the other animals that ate it. Starting in the late 1800s, many states in the Great Plains and Rocky Mountain regions gave a bounty (reward) of between $20 and $50 to people who killed wolves. During this time, some individual wolves, who were given names, became notorious for dodging hunters. Hunters who eventually killed these wolves became famous in their area.

In 1905, at the urging of cattle ranchers, state officials in Montana infected captive wolves with a contagious disease called mange, then sent them back into the wild to infect others. Hunters in Montana also killed more than 80,000 wolves between 1883 and 1918. In 1915, Congress ordered that wolves be removed from all federal lands. The wolf was widely unpopular. President Theodore Roosevelt, a conservationist, called it a "beast of waste and desolation."

By 1935, nearly all gray wolves were gone from the continental United States. A new wave of killing took place in Alaska during the 1940s, when people worried that wolves were killing too many caribou. As wolf packs died out, there were serious consequences. Elk and other game multiplied, and many starved to death. In 1967, the gray wolf was federally listed under the Endangered Species Act in the lower forty-eight states.

While some people killed wolves out of fear, others wanted their skins,

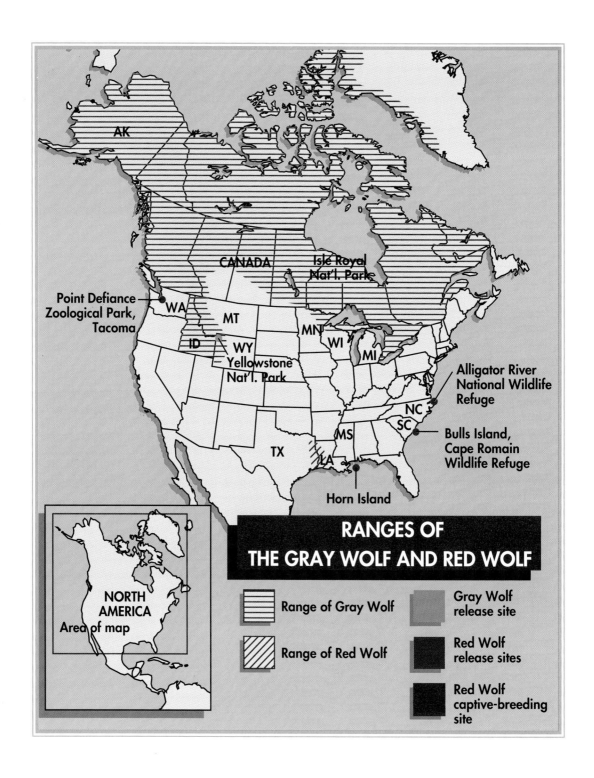

Point Defiance
Zoological Park,
Tacoma

Isle Royal
Nat'l. Park

Alligator River
National Wildlife
Refuge

Bulls Island,
Cape Romain
Wildlife Refuge

Yellowstone
Nat'l. Park

Horn Island

AK

CANADA

WA
MT
ID
WY
MN
WI
MI
NC
SC
MS
TX
LA

RANGES OF
THE GRAY WOLF AND RED WOLF

NORTH
AMERICA
Area of map

Range of Gray Wolf

Range of Red Wolf

Gray Wolf
release site

Red Wolf
release sites

Red Wolf
captive-breeding
site

which they sold for $600 to $700 each. During the 1900s, hunters in Alaska began using ski-equipped planes to find and shoot wolves in remote places. In 1971, Congress passed the Airborne Hunting Act, which made shooting animals from a plane or snowmobile illegal. The major goal of this bill was to protect eagles in western states, but it also helped wolves. Alaskan wolf hunters lobbied for changes in the law, which was amended to allow them to kill wolves from the ground, with rifles, after leaving their planes.

CONSERVATION EFFORTS Attempts to save wolves have been helped by several pieces of legislation, starting with the 1969 National Environmental Protection Act. This act controls the ways in which people can make changes in any species' population or habitat. The Endangered Species Act of 1973 specifically lists endangered species of wolves and gives them some federal protection.

Scientists have studied wolves to see if they threaten humans. The U.S. Fish and Wildlife Service claims that there has never been a confirmed report of a healthy wolf hurting a person in North America. L. David Mech, a wolf biologist, studied cases involving wolves and humans. Numerous people told him that they had observed friendly and harmless wolves. He found that in the vast majority of cases, wolves merely avoid humans. Mech concluded that in cases where wolves had attacked people, they may actually have been going after the people's dogs because wolves view dogs as prey. He also found that people had been bitten after they grabbed wolves, an action that prompts wolves to attack. It appeared also that some aggressive wolves may have had rabies. Mech said, "There is too much evidence that North American wolves are not dangerous to humans. Some nineteen million visitor days with no wolf attacks have been recorded in Minnesota's Superior National Forest alone. . . . The national parks of Canada and Alaska could boast many million more safe visitor days, as could Canada's provincial parks."

Although people have encountered friendly wolves, scientists warn people not to approach wolves in the wild. Packs and individual wolves vary, and an attacking wolf can cause severe injury. Still, Mech says, "The weight of evidence indicates that humans have little to fear from healthy wild wolves."

Some states have found ways to protect both wolves and people. Minnesota has a large wilderness area, but wolves sometimes wander into populated areas and kill livestock. The owners are paid from a special state fund if a wolf kills their cows or sheep. Federal workers trap any wolves that are a problem. Sometimes, these predators turn out to be coyotes, bobcats, or mountain lions rather than wolves. State officials teach ranchers how to keep wolves away—by moving cattle carcasses to places where they will not attract wolves, for example. Ranchers also benefit from laws that allow their animals to graze on public lands at low fees. In Montana, where wolf packs are slowly increasing, a private organization compensates ranchers whose animals are killed by wolves.

In Lake Superior's Isle Royale National Park, a small group of about twenty wolves lives relatively free from interference. Isle Royale is almost 44 miles (71 kilometers) long and is located about 15 miles (24 kilometers) from the nearest mainland shore. Living in the park are fish, more than 200 kinds of birds, and various animals, including moose and caribou, that are hunted by the wolves. The heavily forested island, which has no roads, has been preserved as a wilderness area. People can reach it only by ferry and must roam the island on foot.

New threats to wolves continue to arise. In 1993, Alaska decided to reduce its wolf population. To increase the moose and caribou herds for hunters, hundreds of traps were set up in the Alaska Range to snare wolves. A new law prolonged the hunting season and permitted hunters to use aircraft to spot and track wolves. Airborne hunting is still banned in national parks but is permitted in national wildlife refuges and on other federal lands. A number of people have protested this law. A national park official in Alaska said, "It abandons the principles of fair chase and encourages unethical hunting."

In December 1994, an Alaska television station showed a videotape of some of the results of the trapping program. One trapped wolf had to be shot five times before it finally died. An ensnared pup had chewed off part of its leg while trying to escape. A biologist had made the tape to show people that the traps were inhumane. Public criticism led the state's Fish and Game Commission to announce that it would remove nearly 700 snares from the Alaska Range.

In 1994, an expanded coyote-control program was proposed for southwestern Montana. Besides aerial shootings, officials could use new leg-hold traps, toxic bait, and cyanide-gas ejectors. The National Wildlife Federation and others are opposing the plan, saying it threatens the recovery of gray wolves, who will die along with the coyotes.

RETURNING WOLVES TO FORMER HABITATS   Montana is the scene of another ongoing debate. Wolves have been gone from Yellowstone National Park since the 1930s, the result of extermination by the govern-

ment. In 1963, the National Park Service recommended that national parks re-create as much as possible the conditions that existed before whites settled in America. The Endangered Species Act charges the federal government with the responsibility for carrying out "all methods and procedures necessary" to restore species that face extinction, including restoring wolves to Yellowstone. Surveys conducted during the 1980s showed the public supported the idea by a margin of 6 to 1. Yet, as of 1990, this was yet to be done.

In 1993, however, the government announced a plan to reintroduce wolves to some of their former habitats. Beginning in 1994, fifteen wolves from Canada would be brought to Yellowstone Park and another fifteen to central Idaho every fall for three to five years. These two populations were each expected to reach 100 wolves by the year 2002.

Supporters pointed out that wolves can prevent overpopulation of large game, which numbers about 50,000 in Yellowstone Park. Too many deer, elk, and bison degrade habitats and cause food shortages. When ranchers opposed the plan, the Wolf Fund, the Greater Yellowstone Coalition, and

Not everyone supports the plan to reintroduce wolves to their former habitats. Conservation efforts can affect people's jobs.

other supporters argued that with so much game in the park, the wolves would not need to go outside for food.

Throughout 1993 and 1994, the American Farm Bureau Federation, sheep foundations, and others continued to fight the plan. Addressing their concerns, the U.S. Fish and Wildlife Service promised to kill or move any wolves that repeatedly attacked livestock in the Yellowstone area. Statistics show that in Minnesota, 1,600 wolves co-exist with 20,000 sheep and 232,000 cattle, yet fewer than 110 livestock are killed by wolves each year. In the Greater Yellowstone area, there would be about 100 wolves, 10,000 cows, and 5,000 sheep. Some people also suggest that a buffer zone between the wolves in Yellowstone and the ranches would help to prevent problems.

People who support reintroduction of the wolves believe it would help to make the park "whole" again. If the wolves are returned, Yellowstone will

◆ WOLF LANGUAGE ◆

When people think of wolves, many picture them howling in the night, heads pointed toward the moon. Actually, wolves are more likely to howl in the early evening and early morning than at night. They also howl more often in cold weather, when their sounds echo across the snow- or ice-covered ground. Howling is one way they communicate.

People who study wolves believe they feel a variety of emotions—love, joy, worry, jealousy, and anger. They express their feelings through sounds, facial expressions, and body movements. Howling is a way to "talk" to other pack members before and after a hunt or to warn them of approaching danger. When separated from its group, a lost wolf utters a sad-sounding howl that goes from high to low notes. Wolves also howl when they find themselves in strange surroundings.

Wolves make other sounds besides the howl. They occasionally bark, often in warning and anger. One deep howl followed by barking seems to be the signal for a pack to assemble. Wolves growl when facing enemies or unwelcome visitors, during quarrels, to protect their food, or when they want to be left alone. They also growl to correct a misbehaving pup. Mothers squeak when a pup plays too roughly, and fathers squeak to call a pup. As a rule, whines and squeaks are made during happy times, such as meals.

be the only place in the lower forty-eight states that contains all the native animals and plants that were there when whites came to North America. Wolves are viewed as having as much right to live in Yellowstone as bears or hooved animals. Bringing them back would be an important sign of America's commitment to the environment.

The movement to bring wolves back to their former habitats in state and national parks has spread to Colorado, New Mexico, Arizona, Wyoming, and New York State. In New York, a group called the Adirondack Wolf Project hopes to bring eastern timber wolves to that region. Scott Thiele, who formed the group, echoes the sentiments of those involved in the Yellowstone project when he says, "The wolf gives a mystique to the wilderness. A lot of people just want to know the call of the wild is still out there."

SAVING THE RED WOLF

People have also worked to save red wolves from extinction. The smallest wolves in North America, they weigh from 31 to 81 pounds (14 to 37 kilograms), stand about 15 to 16 inches (38 to 41 centimeters) high, and measure about 70 to 81 inches (178 to 206 centimeters) long, including their tails. Despite the name, their coats are usually dark yellow, gray, or black. Red wolves eat mice, rabbits, and other small prey.

> *RED WOLF*
> *Canis rufus*
>
> **KINGDOM:** Animalia
> **PHYLUM:** Chordata
> **CLASS:** Mammalia
> **ORDER:** Carnivora
> **FAMILY:** Canidae
> **GENUS:** *Canis*
> **SPECIES:** *rufus*

Thousands of these wolves once ranged throughout the low hills and plains of the south-central United States and Gulf coast. As more humans settled these grassland areas, red wolves were shot and poisoned. During the 1880s, a bounty of $20 was offered for their hides. In some places, people mistook them for gray wolves and coyotes, which they feared would attack their livestock. Other red wolves died as a result of hookworms (parasites that live in the intestines) and from heartworms (parasites that cause a fatal disease that strikes canines in the heart; the parasite is spread by mosquitoes living in swamps).

Crossbreeding added to the problem. Through the years, red wolves bred with gray wolves and coyotes, forming mixed breeds. As wolves became scarce, more red wolves mated with coyotes, and their offspring became less like red wolves. By 1973, red wolves had become endangered; in 1975, fewer than a hundred survived.

RED WOLF

The U.S. Fish and Wildlife Service founded a Red Wolf Recovery Team and set up the Red Wolf Captive Breeding Program in 1976. Carefully, scientists searched Texas and Louisiana until they had captured forty true red wolves. They took the wolves to Point Defiance Zoological Park in Tacoma, Washington, where the wolves mated and produced their first litters in 1977. In the years that followed, the wolves were returned to the wild. In preparation, people worked to maintain the wolves' wild instincts so they could survive in their natural habitats without help.

The breeding program placed red wolves on Bulls Island, part of the Cape Romain Wildlife Refuge system in South Carolina; on Horn Island off the Mississippi coast; and in other places. No interbreeding could occur because no coyotes or gray wolves live in these areas. In 1987, eight red wolves (four pairs) were taken to the 120,000-acre (48,000-hectare) Alligator River National Wildlife Refuge in North Carolina. They wore radio transmitters so they could be monitored and located if they strayed onto private lands.

According to the U.S. Fish and Wildlife Department, the red wolf is slowly recovering. There were about 119 true red wolves in the wild and in captivity in 1989. Overall, the breeding program has been a success.

However, decades of crossbreeding between red wolves and gray wolves and coyotes have led people to debate whether today's red wolf is truly a unique species. Biologists have studied DNA (genetic material) from the cells of red wolves, looking for unique traits. If it is proven that red wolves are all hybrids, they could be dropped from the endangered species list. Naturalists have suggested that the Endangered Species Act be changed so that it protects those rare species that have interbred with similar species. This might also affect the Florida panther, which has interbred with cougars.

◆ ◆ ◆

The plight of red and gray wolves shows how animals can die out when people both fear them and see them as competition for the same resources. During recent decades, efforts have been made to reverse the sweeping destruction that government and individuals inflicted on wolves for more than a century. As people have come to appreciate wolves and their role in ecosystems, their future appears brighter.

BLACK-TAILED PRAIRIE DOG

SIX

POISONED ON THE VANISHING PRAIRIE

THE BLACK-TAILED PRAIRIE DOG AND THE BLACK-FOOTED FERRET

Adistinctive feature of the North American landscape is its heartland, a region of vast plains that stretch across the midwestern United States and parts of southern Canada. Before the 1500s, these plains were almost a "sea of grass" covering one-ninth of the continent.

Originally, these grasslands were a shallow inland sea. But over a period of millions of years, sediment washed out of the Rocky Mountains and mixed with silt, sand, clay, and rubble from glaciers (sheets of ice that moved across North America). As a result, the sea became three areas of prairie: a short-grass prairie in the West, a tallgrass area in the East, and a mixed-grass prairie in between. These were the largest grasslands on earth, able to nourish about seventy million bison and fifty million pronghorn antelope along with millions of elk and deer. Coyotes, foxes, badgers, skunks, bobcats, raccoons, birds, and rodents also roamed the prairie, which contained some unique kinds of plants and animals.

Today, natural prairie communities exist only here and there, mostly under national forest service protection. Overhunting, disease, and shrinking habitats have wiped out animals such as the buffalo, Audubon's bighorn sheep, and numerous plants. The prairie dogs that once lived here in the billions have drastically declined in number. In turn, the mountain plovers, burrowing owls, and ferruginous hawks that like to nest in prairie dog areas may soon be endangered. Black-footed ferrets, which depend on prairie dogs for food, are nearly gone from the wild.

BLACK-TAILED PRAIRIE DOG
Cynomys ludovicianus
   KINGDOM: Animalia
   PHYLUM: Chordata
   CLASS: Mammalia
   ORDER: Rodentia
   FAMILY: Sciuridae
   GENUS: *Cynomys*
   SPECIES: *ludovicianus*

SOCIABLE GRASS EATERS Black-tailed prairie dogs (*Cynomys ludovicianus*), short-legged ground squirrels, are about 12 to 17 inches (30 to 40 centimeters) long and weigh 2 to 3 pounds (about 1 to 1.4 kilograms), the size of a small woodchuck. They received their name from American settlers who thought their yaps and chirping sounds resembled the barking of a dog.

These mammals enjoy a community lifestyle in prairie dog towns, located in areas with short grasses. These towns are made up of underground burrows and a system of tunnels. After digging a burrow, the prairie dog surrounds it with an orderly mound of earth. These plump animals can be seen feeding on grass, calling out to one another, or scurrying in and out of their burrows. Prairie dog towns hold about twenty-two burrows per acre (fifty-five burrows per hectare) and may cover hundreds, even thousands, of acres. The largest known town, located in Texas, may have housed around 400 million prairie dogs before the 1800s.

Prairie dog towns teem with life. They attract mice, rabbits, birds, snakes, lizards, toads, salamanders, insects, and spiders. Several prairie dog families live in each colony. Each family, sometimes called a coterie, is made

The vast prairies of North America once provided a feast for prairie dogs.

Prairie dogs are very social animals and enjoy lots of physical contact.

up of one or two males and two or three groups of related female prairie dogs and their young. The males protect these females, who keep strange females away. All of the adults help to feed and rear the pups.

Cooperation is also part of town life and helps the group to survive. Prairie dogs often vocalize, using different sounds in different situations. They take turns acting as "guards" to watch the boundaries of their town. The guards will bark a warning if they spy trespassers or predators, such as eagles, badgers, coyotes, or ferrets. When danger looms, prairie dogs scurry to their holes and jump in headfirst. After a predator leaves, they make other noises that mean it is safe to come out again.

When not building their burrows and tunnels or watching for danger, prairie dogs enjoy a great deal of physical contact. They "groom" fellow members of their community, exchange what looks like a kiss, nibble and stroke each other, and roll around together affectionately. Pups, especially, seem to like this touching.

USEFUL CITIZENS   New prairie dog colonies are built during the springtime, when prairie dogs come out of hibernation to enjoy the fresh green grass shoots and wildflowers. By nibbling the taller grasses, prairie dogs make room for shorter grasses and sprouting seeds. Their digging adds air to the ground, which then holds water better. The soil around their towns grows fertile from the prairie dogs' droppings and from their bones after they die.

Since the food supply around a town may be limited, year-old prairie dogs and some other adults leave their homes during the spring when new pups are born. They build new underground homes and tunnels in a different place with a fresh supply of grasses.

ELUSIVE PREDATORS   The lives of North American, or black-footed, ferrets have been intertwined with those of prairie dogs. Not only do ferrets eat prairie dogs for food, but they make their dens in deserted prairie dog burrows already equipped with deep tunnels and special exit holes for eluding predators. For centuries, ferrets had a range about the same size as that of the prairie dogs, although they were not nearly as numerous.

Ferrets were first described in 1851 by John James Audubon and John Bachman. They classified the animal as *Mustela nigripes*, meaning black-footed mustelid. Mustelidae is a large family that includes the weasel. These quick, graceful animals have round heads, large round ears, and bright greenish-toned eyes. Their pale brown bodies are light underneath, and they have black legs, black tips on their tails, and a distinctive black mask around their eyes. They are about the size of a small mink and may weigh less than the prairie dogs they hunt.

With their sharp teeth and claws, prairie dogs are difficult to catch. A ferret sneaks into their burrows at night in order to take them by surprise. The appearance of a ferret causes terror, and the chattering prairie dogs rush out, pushing dirt from their exit holes.

Those that cannot escape are dragged off to the ferret's den. There, a prairie dog is eaten by a ferret or by a litter of hungry kits, if the hunter was a mother ferret. Kits, born in the spring, can eat meat by the time they are about a week old.

Mother ferrets must hunt but do not like to leave their kits alone for long. Badgers, foxes, coyotes, eagles, and other birds of prey might find the den. At any sign of danger, a mother ferret calls a warning. If she feels unsafe, the mother finds another empty burrow for her kits and may move

BLACK-FOOTED FERRET
Mustela nigripes

KINGDOM:	Animalia
PHYLUM:	Chordata
CLASS:	Mammalia
ORDER:	Carnivora
FAMILY:	Mustelidae
GENUS:	*Mustela*
SPECIES:	*nigripes*

BLACK-FOOTED FERRET

them several times while they are young. In late August, she places each kit in a separate den. She continues to bring them food until they are old enough to hunt for themselves. By fall, when the young go their separate ways, a mother ferret is often weak and thin from the strain of feeding her family all summer.

Although ferrets reduce prairie dog populations a bit, they have never overkilled their prey. Scientists think there have always been only small numbers of ferrets, but they are not sure why. Ferrets stay underground most of the day and hunt at night, so they can be hard to spot. Their tracks show only on mud, snow, or loose dirt, and they rarely leave a trail of droppings. One possible sign of ferrets is a burrow with dirt piled up on its entrance holes. Prairie dogs cover the openings to ferrets' dens in order to trap them inside. The dirt plugs rarely stop ferrets, though, because they are also strong diggers.

For years, scientists considered black-footed ferrets to be rare and mysterious. At the turn of the century, there were fewer than a dozen ferret specimens in museums. In 1929, naturalist Ernest Thompson Seton found so few recorded ferret sightings that he said the animal might be gone. By then, ranchers were trying to destroy prairie dogs, and Dr. Seton wrote, "Now that the Demon of Commerce has declared war on the prairie-dog, that merry little simpleton of the Plains must go . . . and with the passing of the Prairie-dog, the Ferret, too, will pass."

COMPETING FOR THE GRASSLANDS   By the late 1800s, western settlers had come to view prairie dogs and their towns as a nuisance. Prairie dog towns stretched across some 600,000 square miles (1.6 million square kilometers) of prairie—land the ranchers wanted free for their grazing animals. As this land gave way to roads, homes, farms, and ranches, the wildlife had to change its ways, find new homes, or die.

Ranchers claimed that the prairie dogs ate grass their cattle needed and that horses often tripped on the loose earth and holes around prairie dog burrows. The issue became more involved as people argued about how much forage the prairie dogs ate in comparison to what cattle ate. Then scientists began to wonder if overgrazing by livestock caused the prairie dogs to spread out more, to places where the prairie grasses were cut low enough for them to reach easily.

Starting around 1880, private citizens lobbied to get rid of the prairie dogs, which then numbered about five billion. In the 1900s, the U.S. gov-

THE OLD WAYS OF THE GRASSLANDS

For centuries, the plants and animals of the grass-land ecosystem have depended upon each other for life. Years ago, the buffalo played an important role in the life cycle of both the prairie dog and the ferret. Buffalo grazed on the prairie, clearing enough land so that prairie dogs could move in to dig their underground burrows. This digging aerated the soil, which was then fertilized by the prairie dogs' droppings. Prairie dogs cut the grass short in order to maintain a clear

The arrival of the railroad signaled the beginning of the end for buffalo on the prairie.

view of their surroundings. Grasses like blue grama and little bluestem sprouted longer, in a stage of growth that nourished other animals. Bison and pronghorn antelope came to graze on them.

Black-footed ferrets, badgers, weasels, and rattlesnakes ate weak or sick prairie dogs, reducing their numbers. Prairie dog towns attracted buffalo who came to wallow—roll around—in the dirt in order to remove insects and loose hair from their coats. As buffalo tore up their old towns, prairie dogs relocated and built new ones. Ferrets, ground squirrels, voles, and other animals made homes in deserted prairie dog burrows. Soon, fresh grass carpeted the abandoned dog towns, and a new life cycle began.

Once the buffalo were gone from the prairie in the late 1800s, this delicate balance was destroyed. The stage was set for massive overgrowth of prairie dog towns, distressing white settlers who then proceeded to poison millions of prairie dogs, endangering black-footed ferrets at the same time.

ernment joined a massive effort to poison prairie dogs, using strychnine and Compound 1090. People pumped poison gas into prairie dog towns, also killing ferrets and other animals that lived there. More animals died when they ate poisoned prairie dog corpses. By the early 1970s, people were poisoning more than 250,000 acres (100,000 hectares) of prairie a year.

By 1993, the population of prairie dogs in North America had been reduced by more than 90 percent. The Utah prairie dog was threatened and the Mexican prairie dog was endangered. Prairie dogs were no longer such a common sight in the West, although some colonies remained in national parks and on private property. While the dogs seemed sturdy enough to recover, black-footed ferrets were on the verge of extinction.

SAVING PREY AND PREDATOR

In an effort to save prairie dogs and ferrets, scientists studied both animals more carefully. They disputed the idea that prairie dogs deprive cattle of food, saying that the prairie dogs usually eat no more than 7 percent of the forage in a pasture. Studies showed that cattle gain about the same amount of weight in prairie dog areas as they do elsewhere. Wildlife supporters explained how prairie dogs improve the quality of the soil and vegetation. Even so, ranchers continued to kill them. Some people, including children, have been seen killing prairie dogs for entertainment or for target-shooting practice.

To save prairie dogs from extinction, national parks have established safe areas for them. As of the early 1990s, one small prairie dog town remained in a national park in southern Saskatchewan, Canada. In the United States, there are protected areas for prairie dogs in Wyoming, Oklahoma, and South Dakota.

Saving ferrets has been far more difficult. Those ferrets that survived poisoning or disease lost their food supply and habitats and had trouble finding mates. By the mid-1900s, the U.S. Fish and Wildlife Service realized that its pest-control program against prairie dogs was causing ferrets to become extinct. Black-footed ferrets appeared on the first list of endangered animals put out by the Department of the Interior in 1947. Describing the department's dilemma, officials made this statement: "The Department has the responsibility for protecting rare and endangered species and also to control animals significantly detrimental to the best interests of man."

In practice, these two jobs were in conflict. Field agents could not determine where ferrets lived in order to avoid placing poison there. Agents spent many nights using searchlights to scan thousands of acres for a glimpse of a ferret. The National Park Service decided to study the ferret's range. Field officers sighted some sixty ferrets between 1948 and 1952. About one-third of them were dead, and the rest were living in prairie dog towns set for extermination. One official suggested that some ferrets be trapped and relocated in protected prairie dog towns in national parks. The plan failed and was not repeated. *The Vanishing Prairie*, a 1953 nature film by Disney Studios, featured the story of five ferrets that were found in South Dakota. One died in a trap, and one died from a prior gunshot wound. Of the three survivors, two escaped as they were being taken to Wind Cave National Park in South Dakota. The other was released in the park, but no ferrets were seen there in the following years.

In the 1960s, a park service biologist, Walter Kittams, tried to interest people in saving black-footed ferrets. To begin his project, he investigated sightings of ferrets, dead or alive. He and other scientists visited numerous prairie dog towns to find ferrets and to talk to ranchers nearby. In all, the scientists recorded only twenty-nine sightings between 1960 and 1964, and four of these ferrets were dead.

By this time, scientists feared that all black-footed ferrets were gone, but in South Dakota, field agents for the National Park Service, which had been trying to capture some ferrets to place in parks where they might breed, found a mother ferret with four young. Biologist F. Robert Henderson said, "The existence of the black-footed ferret was now official. I hoped this would stir up the Bureau [of Fish and Wildlife] in Washington to do something to protect the species. As for me, I was greatly excited. I knew I had seen one of the rarest and most mysterious little mammals in the world—one that had hardly been studied at all. I decided I'd study it myself—on my own time, if necessary."

Henderson did go on to study black-footed ferrets and their habits. He and other scientists worked to interest the government in plans to save this species from extinction. By 1964, more detailed plans to protect endangered wildlife were being developed by the Bureau of Sport Fisheries and Wildlife, which was legally obliged to protect any black-footed ferrets that were found. This conflicted with its pest-control project against prairie dogs, a situation that has arisen with other animals whose lives are closely related.

However, public attitudes were shifting toward the idea that wildlife should be conserved for future generations. People began to value various

Photographs of ferrets in the wild are almost as rare as ferrets themselves!

Former range of the
Black-footed Ferret and
Black-tailed Prairie Dog

Ferret release sites

Ferret captive-
breeding sites

Protected area
for Prairie Dogs

**RANGE OF THE BLACK-FOOTED FERRET
AND BLACK-TAILED PRAIRIE DOG**

plants and animals, not only for their role in the balance of nature but because they realized that each species is irreplaceable and therefore has an inherent value. The Bureau of Sport Fisheries and Wildlife made a renewed effort not to poison prairie dog towns where ferrets lived. During the 1970s, when many prairie dogs were still being killed, conservationists tried to convince officials to delay or avoid poisoning a town until they were convinced no ferrets lived there.

Even so, in 1980, scientists once again feared that there were no ferrets left in the wild. An occasional sighting in the early 1980s proved that some had survived, but, by then, black-footed ferrets were considered the most endangered animals in North America. Wildlife officials managed to cap-

Captive breeding of ferrets seems to be the last hope of preventing their extinction.

ture some, attaching radio-transmitter collars to their necks so their movements could be tracked.

In 1983, it was decided to breed some ferrets in captivity and then return them to the wild. It was clear that many ferrets were dying of distemper and having trouble finding mates. Scientists planned to capture ferrets in Wyoming and bring them to a research facility in Patuxent, Maryland, where they would breed them to develop a wider gene pool. They planned to release the ferrets into separate colonies so that disease and other hazards could not wipe out so much of the population at once.

The scientists faced many obstacles in catching the animals and, later, several of the captive ferrets died of distemper. The researchers decided to trap all the black-footed ferrets they could find and bring them to Maryland, where they would be safer. The ferrets at the research facility were separated from one another to prevent disease from spreading.

In 1987, the research team received twelve Siberian ferrets, close relatives of the black-footed type, from Russia and from various locations around the United States. They bred these ferrets with eighteen from Wyoming for several years, then established new colonies in Virginia, Nebraska, and Wyoming. In Wyoming, some of the ferrets starved or were eaten by predators, but about twenty were still alive as of 1992, and some had given birth to healthy young.

Scientists planned to continue the breeding program until there were several hundred breeding pairs of black-footed ferrets in different parts of the world. As in the case of some other endangered animals, humans had found it necessary to intervene with scientific tools and strategies in order to reverse the harm that had been done to the animals in previous years.

SEVEN

On the Brink of Extinction

FLORIDA PANTHERS

*T*hroughout the world, members of the cat family are in trouble. Most of the thirty-seven species in this animal family are either threatened or endangered. As wilderness areas have been developed for human use, the big cats have lost their homes. They have also been killed for their fur and because people feared them.

Florida panthers are a subspecies of cougar (the species *Felis concolor*). Once, cougars, pumas, catamounts, and mountain lions (all names for the same species) roamed over a large range in the Western Hemisphere, stretching from the southern end of South America north into most of the United States and Canada. Today, these wild cats are found only in deserts, rain forests, mountains, and other wilderness areas.

ROOTS IN THE WESTERN HEMISPHERE   Long ago, the Florida panther ranged throughout the southeastern United States from Texas, the lower Mississippi valley, through the panhandle of Florida, to the Everglades, and up the Atlantic Coast to South Carolina and Tennessee. Today, there are a mere thirty to fifty of these big cats living in protected areas of southern Florida, south of Lake Okeechobee, around the Everglades and Big Cypress Swamp regions.

Panthers have lived in Florida for at least 500 years. Scientists digging up swamp areas have found ancient statues of what look like panther gods or panther men carved by the Calusa Indians of Key Marco. Scientific tests showed that these figures date back to between A.D. 1400 and 1500. But panthers probably lived in this region earlier, as did other cougars in the Americas.

MUSCULAR MEAT EATERS

The panthers that became isolated in southern Florida developed unique traits. They are smaller than western cougars, measuring about 7 feet (2.1 meters) in length and weighing from 106 to 148 pounds (48 to 67 kilograms). Males average 130 pounds (59 kilograms), while females weigh between 60 and 80 pounds (27 to 36 kilograms). Their noses are broad and flat with arched nostrils. Florida panthers have longer legs than other cougars and sport a distinctive swirl of fur, called a cowlick, down the middle of their backs. Their tails turn upward at the end where three bones are bent. Their short, rather stiff fur is a slightly darker shade of tan than is the fur of some cougars and helps them to blend in with deer, their major prey.

These carnivores (meat-eating animals) need large amounts of food to survive. It takes thirty-five to fifty deer-sized animals a year to feed an adult panther and more than that to sustain a female who is raising a litter. Panthers eat mainly large prey, such as deer, but will eat smaller animals— wild hogs, raccoons, rabbits, cotton rats, birds, even grasshoppers—if nothing else is available. The panthers may have to hunt throughout a large area and spend several hours stalking their prey before they can finally make a kill.

NEW LIFE

Pregnant female panthers prepare their dens in dry, sheltered places that will not be noticed by predators. In the Florida wilderness, the middle of a palmetto thicket is a desirable site. The heavy leaves shield the litter from intense sun and rain while hiding the family from view. A typical litter contains one to four kittens, each weighing about 1 pound (0.45 kilogram) at birth. The mother raises her young by herself. Males live alone except when mating, and females live alone except when rearing their young.

A mother panther must leave her young to hunt for food but tries to return as soon as possible. Hawks and other predators are a constant danger. She must also protect the young from other panthers, for adult males kill and eat young panthers as large as 50 pounds (23 kilograms). When her offspring are about two years old, the mother takes them out with her and kills

A panther cub stays with its mother for almost two years.

prey for them to eat. She then leaves them and prepares to mate again. Each young panther establishes its own territory, or home range.

The lifestyle of the Florida panther requires a large amount of space because they live alone and need a certain number of deer. It is estimated that they need about 116 square miles (302 square kilometers) per animal. Females may share a range, but males do not. They need a range that includes several female panthers with which to mate. Females like to establish a den near an area with white-tailed deer and other prey so that they can find enough food to feed their kittens without leaving them for too long.

THREATS TO SURVIVAL   Florida panthers have faced several threats to their survival. In 1832, fearing panthers were dangerous to humans, the territorial legislature of Florida passed a law that gave people a bounty for killing them. By 1887, this amount had reached $5 for each panther scalp.

In addition, during the 1900s, as more and more people came to Florida and built homes, farms, and groves, panthers had to keep moving south into the few remaining uninhabited areas. They gravitated to swamp areas because wetlands are one of their favored habitats. But the clearing of land continued, along with the draining of more swamp areas. Water was diverted from wetlands to populated areas where people wanted irrigation.

Wilderness areas have continued to decrease in size during the twentieth century. As land was taken over for citrus groves and other crops, panthers have been left homeless. They have been isolated from their prey and from potential mates, resulting in fewer new panthers. Young panthers may need weeks or months to find a territory that has not already been taken by an adult panther. Some fortunate few are able to assume the former range of a dead panther, but many die of starvation or other causes before they find a safe place to live. Meanwhile, the human population of Florida continues to increase, from some four million in the 1960s to fourteen million by the early 1990s. Most people settle in the popular southern Florida region, where panthers traditionally lived.

An example of how development hurts wildlife occurred in the early 1960s, when State Road 84 was built across Florida. The road, nicknamed "Alligator Alley," cut across the Everglades and passed through the Fakahatchee Strand State Preserve and Big Cypress National Preserve, where Florida panthers and other endangered animals live.

Between 1979 and 1989, twelve panthers were killed by cars or trucks on southwest Florida roads, five of them on Alligator Alley. Since the road cut across their range, the panthers had to cross it to hunt and to mate. Motorists did not see the panthers on the road at night.

The panthers also faced a dwindling food supply. Deer in the region were blamed for causing a widespread tick infestation of local cattle. When numerous deer were killed to stop ticks from spreading, the panthers suffered.

They have also had numerous breeding problems. Besides the difficulty of finding mates in their isolated patches of habitat, male panthers have been found to be less fertile (able to father offspring) than in previous years. It is believed that pollution of the land and water with pesticides and toxic chemicals has damaged their reproductive organs. Some genetic abnormalities have been blamed on the fact that panthers have become so inbred during recent decades. With fewer mates available, they mate with relatives. There is now less diversity among members of their species, which can weaken offspring.

CONSERVATION EFFORTS By 1950, people had noticed that panthers seemed to shy away from contact with humans and might not be dangerous. At that time, the panther was considered a game species, and hunting was restricted to open deer season. In 1958, Florida panthers were

*R*oad signs warn drivers to be alert when they are traveling in areas where panthers live.

removed from the game list and protected from hunting by law, although illegal hunting continues to this day.

Panthers were formally listed in the federal Endangered Species Act of 1973. The loss of their habitats was considered to be the main threat to their continued existence. The U.S. Fish and Wildlife Service formed the Panther Recovery Team in 1976. The team studied panthers in the wild and developed a plan to save them from extinction. Two years later, the state legislature passed the Florida Panther Act, which made killing these animals a felony.

Supporters of endangered animals protested when the state announced plans to expand the road called Alligator Alley to four lanes. The Florida Game and Fresh Water Fish Commission and the U.S. Fish and Wildlife Service came up with a plan to build underpasses so that animals could cross under the highway at their customary places. By tracking the movements of animals wearing radio-transmitter collars, officials determined where to build the underpasses. The first finished underpass, for the use of animals only, was 8 feet (2.4 meters) tall and 100 feet (30 meters) wide. Fences were erected along the road to steer animals toward the underpasses so they would use them.

In 1982, the panther was made the official state animal of Florida, which increased public awareness of its plight. There were articles and news

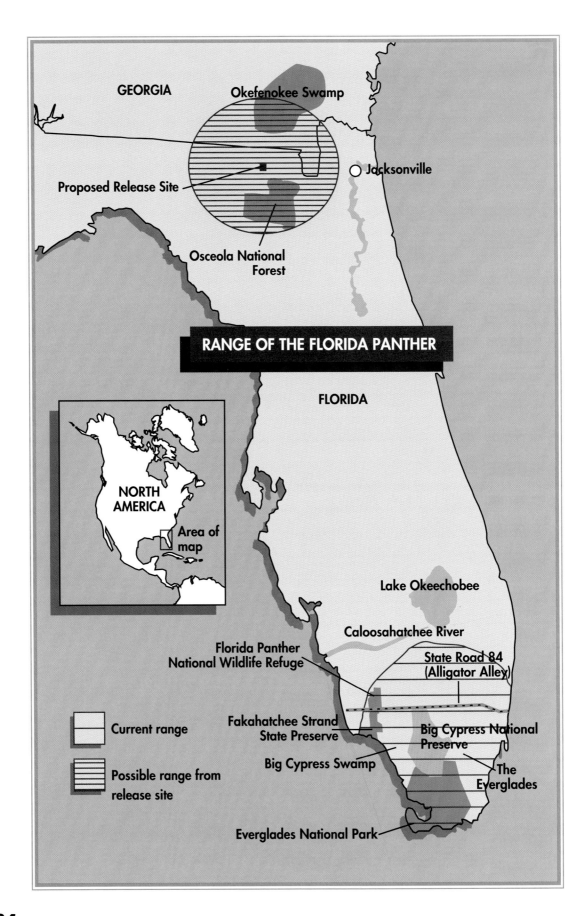

GEORGIA

Okefenokee Swamp

Proposed Release Site

○ Jacksonville

Osceola National
Forest

RANGE OF THE FLORIDA PANTHER

FLORIDA

NORTH
AMERICA

Area of
map

Lake Okeechobee

Caloosahatchee River

Florida Panther
National Wildlife Refuge

State Road 84
(Alligator Alley)

Fakahatchee Strand
State Preserve

Big Cypress National
Preserve

Big Cypress Swamp

The
Everglades

Current range

Possible range from
release site

Everglades National Park

programs describing the danger of extinction. Two new agencies were formed: the Florida Panther Technical Advisory Council and the Florida Panther Interagency Committee. The recovery team, which was still at work, included representatives from the Game and Fresh Water Fish Commission, the Department of Natural Resources, the Florida Audubon Society, the U.S. National Park Service, and the Rare Feline Breeding Center. The team had undertaken some costly and ambitious programs to save the panthers.

In 1989, the U.S. Fish and Wildlife Service set up a 30,000-acre (12,000-hectare) Florida Panther National Wildlife Refuge. It was hoped that this protected area, including favorable habitats for panthers, would allow some to survive and breed.

Teams of scientists also set out to study the panther more extensively in order to find more ways to help it survive. Although it is one of the most endangered mammals in the world, little is known about the animal. They are hard to locate in the wild, where they easily blend in with their surroundings and find ample hiding places in remote areas. Scientists have used dogs to track panthers down so that they can tag them with radio-transmitter collars.

It is estimated that most adult Florida panthers, only about twenty-two to twenty-five in number now, have been collared. Collared animals are tracked throughout the year. They receive medical care when health problems are suspected and can be regularly vaccinated to prevent distemper and certain other diseases. At times, a collarless panther (a newborn or one that has never been tagged) is spotted in the wild. Experts can guess they are around by the sight of their tracks, droppings on the ground, or the remains of their killed prey.

BREEDING FOR SURVIVAL   A captive breeding program for panthers was approved in 1990. Biologists were able to find three male and three female kittens with very different genes. A great deal of planning followed. A team of biologists, working at a facility north of Jacksonville, decided to breed the animals during cool weather because that appeared to be less stressful to them.

The goal of this program is to release healthy offspring into the wild by the year 2001. Scientists will be careful to help the animals keep enough wild traits to survive in the wilderness. This means minimizing the animals' contact with people and keeping the grounds of the facility as natural as possible. An ongoing captive-breeding program is viewed as crucial to the panther's survival.

Another, more controversial plan for the panthers is to breed them with cougars outside their own subspecies, perhaps western cougars. Some supporters of interbreeding claim it is the only real hope for Florida panthers, but there is opposition to the plan. Opponents worry that this new breed might not adapt well to conditions in Florida. Another fear is that if the Florida panther becomes a hybrid (a mixed breed) of panther, it will lose its status as a subspecies protected by federal law. But the laws could be changed so that panthers in Florida would continue to receive protection.

Since the loss of habitat has been such a problem for the panther, conservationists want to acquire more land for their use and improve their present habitat. More deer can be brought to an area through the burning of specific stands of trees by experts. This exposes the ground to more sunlight, encouraging more of the low-growing vegetation that deer eat. Among the new lands being acquired is a 40,000-acre (16,000-hectare) wildlife refuge in Collier County, Florida. Two other tracts, each more than 400,000 acres (160,000 hectares) large, north and south of the Caloosahatchee River, are also viewed as critical habitat for the panthers.

Because panthers need a broad range in order to survive, there are also plans to reintroduce the panthers into two large areas that border Florida and Georgia: the Osceola National Forest and Okefenokee Swamp. In 1994, eight radio-collared Texas cougars were released into the Osceola National Forest. Scientists expected them to mate with Florida panthers, since both animals are subspecies of the same species. This would strengthen the gene pool of the panthers, which have had few breeding partners in recent decades.

◆ ◆ ◆

The Florida panther, a symbol of the state's special landscape, may already be extinct. By 1994, it was unclear if more than fifty panthers, counting both adult and young panthers, remained in the wild. Their problems—killing by humans, dwindling habitats, a reduced food supply, and barriers to successful mating and breeding—are shared by many other endangered species. If people succeed in saving the panthers, their efforts may provide a model for saving large cats and other animals throughout the world.

Challenges for the Future

*T*oday, more than five billion people share an ever more crowded earth with other forms of life. By the year 2000, there may be 6.25 billion people wanting food, water, homes, furniture, energy, clothing, roads, and schools, as well as other things many people enjoy: cars, televisions, toasters, hair dryers, magazines, sports equipment, toys—a seemingly endless list. This will put increasing strains on resources and animal habitats.

Around the world, concerned people are working to save threatened animals and plants, as well as the land, water, and air on which life depends. Governments are making long-term plans for the use of natural resources. International meetings are held regularly, and the years 1990 to 2000 have been named the Decade of the Environment.

Individuals can help by conserving water and fuel, recycling papers and garbage, using car pools, demanding biodegradable packaging materials, and supporting laws that protect the natural environment. Fast-food restaurants have been among the businesses that responded to customer requests by replacing plastic Styrofoam packaging with paper.

Young people have been active supporters of the environment. Most schools now include programs about the environment encouraging students to become involved in preserving it. Some young people have joined groups that collect cans, bottles, and newspapers and other paper products that can be recycled. Many schools have special recycling bins for materials left over from lunch boxes and papers that have been used at school or at home. Schools also organize programs to improve the environment. Groups of students have written letters to various food and beverage manufacturers urging them to use recycled materials and to reduce the amount of packaging around their products. In some towns, teams of students have taken part in cleanup days, during which they collect debris around lakes and streams. College students have distributed educational materials about environmental causes door to door.

These efforts and others may help to save some of the world's endangered plants and animals from extinction. In the past, some endangered animals have been saved. Others are gone, never to be seen again. Among the mammals of the world that became extinct during the past two centuries are the Atlas bear, Cape lion, Antarctic wolf, Gilbert's rat kangaroo, Barbary lion, Rufou gazelle, white-tailed rat, long-eared kit fox, quagga (a type of zebra), sea mink, and Stellar's sea cow (a relative of the manatee). Will one or more of today's endangered mammals join this list? Scientists believe that even with some conservation efforts, about one-fifth of the life forms on earth today will be lost by the year 2024.

Nothing can bring back a lost species, and nobody knows for certain what is lost when an animal or a plant vanishes forever. Today more than ever, people realize the connections among living things and the valuable roles played by life in all its shapes and sizes. Plants and animals now extinct might have provided humans with important scientific information, medicines, and food, as well as contributing their unique form and traits to the earth. Through the years, thoughtful people have warned that all life forms on earth are interwoven in ways that we cannot fully understand. Nearly 150 years ago, Chief Seattle of the Suquamish tribe of the Pacific Northwest said, "Man did not weave the web of life, he is merely a strand in it. Whatever he does to the web, he does to himself."

Although much has already been lost, humans have managed to save endangered animals in the past; making the planet a healthier place for all is the key to saving others in the future.

FOR FURTHER READING

Amazing Animals of the Sea. Washington, DC: National Geographic Society, 1981.

Banks, Martin. *Endangered Wildlife*. Vero Beach, Fla.: Rourke Enterprises, 1988.

Brown, Michael, and John May. *The Greenpeace Story: The Inside Story of the World's Most Dynamic Environmental Group*. New York: Dorling Kindersley, 1989.

Burt, Olive W. *Rescued: America's Endangered Wildlife on the Comeback Trail*. Englewood Cliffs, New Jersey: Julian Messner, 1980.

Cadieux, Charles. *These Are the Endangered*. San Jose: Stone Walled Press, 1981.

Casey, Denise. *The Black Footed Ferret*. New York: Dodd, Mead, 1985.

Clark, Margaret Goff. *The Endangered Florida Panther*. New York: Dutton, 1993.

Drump, Donald, ed. *National Geographic Books of Mammals*. Washington, DC: National Geographic Society, 1981.

Emanoil, Mary, ed. *Encyclopedia of Endangered Species*. Detroit: Gale Research, 1994.

Goodman, Billy. *A Kid's Guide to How to Save the Animals*. New York: Avon Camelot, 1991.

Gutfreund, Geraldine Marshall. *Vanishing Animal Neighbors*. New York: Franklin Watts, 1993.

Javna, John. *50 Simple Things Kids Can Do to Save the Earth*. Kansas City: Andrews and McMeel, 1990.

Lawrence, R. D. *Wolves*. New York: Little, Brown, 1990.

MacDonald, John. *Encyclopedia of Mammals*. New York: Facts On File, 1984.

Martin, Richard Mark. *Mammals of the Oceans*. New York: G. P. Putnam's Sons, 1977.

Matthews, John R., and Charles J. Moseley, eds. *The Official World Wildlife Fund Guide to Endangered Species of North America*. Washington, DC: Beacham, 1990.

Maynard, Thane. *Endangered Animal Babies: Saving Species One Birth at a Time*. New York: Franklin Watts, 1993.

Patent, Dorothy Hinshaw. *Habitats: Saving Wild Places*. Hillside, New Jersey: Enslow, 1993.

Pringle, Laurence. *Batman: Exploring the World of Bats*. New York: Charles Scribner's Sons, 1991.

———. *Wolfman*. New York: Charles Scribner's Sons, 1984.

Stefoff, Rebecca. *Extinction*. New York: Chelsea House, 1992.

Time-Life Books. *Whales and Other Sea Mammals*. New York: Charles Scribner's Sons, 1976.

Unterbrink, Mary. *Manatees—Gentle Giants in Peril*. St. Petersburg, Fla.: Great Outdoors Publishing Co., 1984.

Whitfield, Philip *Can the Whales Be Saved? Questions About the Natural World and*

Threats to Its Survival Answered by the Natural History Museum. New York: Viking Kestrel, 1989.

MAGAZINES:

AUDUBON:
Isbell, Connie M. "The Battle for Mount Graham," July/August 1993, 110–111.
Laycock, George. "How to Kill a Wolf," November 1990, 44–48.
Madson, John. "Dark Days in Dogtown," 70:32–43 (1968).
Mech, L. David. "Who's Afraid of the Big Bad Wolf?" March 1990, 82–85.
Williams, Ted. "Waiting for Wolves to Howl in Yellowstone," November 1990, 32–41.

NATIONAL GEOGRAPHIC:
Balog, James. "A Personal Vision of Vanishing Wildlife," April 1990, 84–103.
Chadwick, Douglas H. "The American Prairie: Roots of the Sky," October 1993, 90–119.
Farney, Dennis. "The Tallgrass Prairie: Can It Be Saved?" January 1980, 37–61.
Hall, Alice J. "Man and Manatee: Can We Live Together?" September 1984, 400–413.
Hartman, Daniel S. "Florida's Manatees: Mermaids in Peril," September 1969, 342–353.
Novick, Alvin. "Bats Aren't All Bad," May 1973, 615–637.
White, Jesse R. "Man Can Save the Manatee," September 1984, 414–418.
Zahl, Paul A. "Portrait of a Fierce and Fragile Land," (Alaskan Tundra), March 1972, 303–336. "Mammals of the Alaskan Tundra," 329–335.

NATURAL HISTORY:
Mohlenbrock, Robert H. "Mount Graham, Arizona," March 1987, 89–90.
Novacek, Michael J. "Navigators of the Night," October 1988, 67–70.

SCIENTIFIC AMERICAN:
Gittleman, John L., and Robert K. Wayne. "The Problematic Red Wolf, " July 1995.
O'Shea, Thomas J. "Manatees," July 1994, 50–56.

SMITHSONIAN:
Scheffer, V. B. "The Last Days of the Sea Cow," March 1973, 64–67.
Tuttle, Merlin D. "Harmless, Highly Beneficial, Bats Still Get a Bum Rap," January 1984, 74–81.
Vietmeyer, Noel. "The Endangered But Useful Manatee," December 1974, 60–64.

PLACES TO VISIT

Babcock Wilderness Adventure, 8000 Route 31, Punta Gorda, FL 33982; phone 1–813–639–4488. Operates tours by swamp buggy over the 90,000-acre ranch, where panthers can be observed living in the wild within a fenced area.

Buffalo Gap National Grassland (U.S. Forest Service), 209 North River Street, Hot Springs, SD 57747; phone 1–605–745–4107. Prairie dog colonies can be found on the thousands of acres of grasslands here.

Congress Avenue Bridge, downtown Austin, TX. This habitat for free-tail bats includes an observation area and educational exhibit.

Fort Niobrara National Wildlife Refuge, Hidden Timber Route, HC 14, Box 67, Valentine, NE 69201; phone 1–402–376–3789. Prairie dogs can be seen in their colonies in this protected setting.

Jungle Larry's Zoological Park at Caribbean Gardens, 1590 Goodlette Road, Naples, FL 33940; phone 1–813–262–5409. Home to nearly 200 animals including 50 species, some endangered.

Monterey Bay Aquarium, 886 Cannery Row, Monterey, CA 93940; phone 1–408–648–4888. Exhibits in the Hall of Marine Mammals include life-sized models of two gray whales and two orcas; live sea mammals at the aquarium include seals, sea lions, and sea otters.

National Zoological Park, 3001 Connecticut Avenue N.W., Washington, DC 20008; phone 1–202–673–4955. Contains exhibits dealing with endangered mammals and other endangered animals; live exhibits include a black-footed ferret, black-tailed prairie dogs, and numerous types of bats.

Octagon Wildlife Sanctuary, 41660 Horseshoe Road, Punta Gorda, FL 33955; phone 1–813–543–1130. A sanctuary and rehabilitative center for animals. Animals capable of living in the wild are returned to their habitats. One Florida panther who lost his tail after being hit by a car has lived here since 1992.

Sea World, 7007 Sea World Drive, Orlando, FL 32821; phone 1–407– 363–2613. A permanent exhibit called "Manatees: The Lost Generation" includes several manatees in a Florida freshwater-spring setting. The manatees, which change regularly, are usually orphans rescued by a Sea World recovery team.

Tallahassee Museum of History and Natural Science, 3945 Museum Drive, Tallahassee, FL 32310; phone 1–904–576–1636. Includes a children's museum, discovery center, and live exhibits of animals in natural habitats.

Wind Cave National Park, Route 1, Box 190, Hot Springs, SD 57747; phone 1–605–745–4600. Prairie dog towns can be observed on the grounds of this national park.

ORGANIZATIONS TO CONTACT

American Cave Conservation Association, P.O. Box 409, Horse Cave, KY 42749; phone 1–502–786–1466. Can send information about the group's work to protect and preserve caves and endangered species, including bats living in the caves.

Arizona Game and Fish Department, Wildlife Management Division, 2222 West Greenway Road, Phoenix, AZ 85023–4399; phone 1–602–942–3000. Can send information about the Mount Graham red squirrel and other wildlife in the region.

Bat Conservation International, P.O. Box 162603, Austin, TX 78716; phone 1–512–327–9721. Provides information about different bats and efforts to save them throughout the world.

Bureau of Land Management, Wildlife and Fisheries Division, 1849 C Street N.W., Washington, DC 20240; phone 1–202–452–7770. Provides information and other materials about conservation and saving wildlife habitats, as well as commercial fishing.

Center For Environmental Information, 50 West Main Street, Rochester, NY 14614; phone 1–716–262–2870. Provides information about environmental issues, laws, and changes taking place in the global environment.

The Center for Marine Conservation (Educational Materials), 1725 De Sales Street N.W., Washington, DC 20036; phone 1–202–429–5609. Can send information about its efforts to prevent marine pollution and save endangered marine species and their habitat.

Defenders of Wildlife, 1101 14th Street N.W., Washington, DC 20005; phone 1–202–682–9400. Provides educational materials about their efforts to protect wildlife and habitats, including fact sheets on different marine mammals, newsletters, and lists of slide shows.

Environmental Defense Fund, 257 Park Avenue South, New York, NY 10010; phone 1–212–505–2100. Provides information about air and water pollution, recycling efforts, and other environmental issues.

Florida Game and Fresh Water Fish Commission, 620 South Meridian Street, Tallahassee, FL 32399–1600; phone 1–904–488–4676. Can provide information about the manatee and the Florida panther (including captive breeding program, the Florida Panther Research and Management Trust Fund, and the Florida Panther Interagency Committee).

Florida Marine Research Institute, Division of Marine Resources, 100 Eighth Avenue S.E., St. Petersburg, FL 33701–5095; phone 1–813–896–8626. Provides information about the manatee and Florida panther.

Florida Power and Light Company, Environmental Affairs, P.O. Box 14000, Juno

Beach, FL 33408; phone 1–800–552–8440. Call or write for illustrated pamphlets and other information about the manatee and the Florida panther.

Florida Wildlife Federation, P.O. Box 6870, Tallahassee, FL 32314; phone 1–904–656–7113. Can supply information about the manatee and Florida panther, as well as other wildlife in the region.

Greater Yellowstone Coalition, P.O. Box 1874, Bozeman, MT 59771; phone 1–406–586–1593. Provides information about the gray wolf and conservation efforts in the Yellowstone area.

Greenpeace, USA, 1436 U Street N.W., Washington, DC 20009; phone 1–202–462–1177. Can provide information on the marine environment and endangered whales.

National Audubon Society, 700 Broadway, New York, NY 10003; phone 1–212–979–3000. Provides educational materials about endangered mammals and about the Mount Graham Coalition and other conservation projects.

National Endangered Species Act Reform Coalition, 1050 Thomas Jefferson Street N.W., Washington, DC 20007; phone 1–202–333–7481.

National Wildlife Federation, 1400 16th Street N.W., Washington, DC 20036–2266; phone 1–202–797–6800. Provides information about endangered animals and efforts to save them; ways for young people to help.

National Zoological Park, 3001 Connecticut Avenue N.W., Washington, DC 20008; phone 1–202–673–4955. Can provide information about the park's research on zoo-based conservation.

The Nature Conservancy, 1815 North Lynn Street, Arlington, VA 22209; phone 1–703–841–5300. This organization is dedicated to buying and protecting habitats; write or call for information.

Save the Manatee Club, 500 North Maitland Avenue, Maitland, FL 33751; phone 1–800–432–5646. Provides information about manatees and the efforts being made to save them, including the "Adopt-a-Manatee" and "Adopt-a-Refuge" programs.

Sierra Club, 730 Polk Street, San Francisco, CA 94109; phone 1–415–776–2211. Provides information about programs to educate the public about environmental issues and legislation that affects the environment (for example, laws regarding air quality and toxic waste disposal).

U.S. Fish and Wildlife Service, Division of Law Enforcement, P.O. Box 3247, Arlington, VA 22203–3247; phone 1–703–358–1949. Provides information about endangered species and laws relating to wildlife.

Wildlife Conservation International, Building A, New York Zoological Society, Bronx, NY 10460; phone 1–718–220–5097. This organization can provide information about its work to protect biological diversity by saving animals and their habitats, especially key species in valuable habitats.

World Wildlife Fund, 1250 24th Street N.W., Suite 400, Washington, DC 20037; phone 1–202–293–4800. Provides information about endangered animals and their habitats, conservation laws and programs, and illegal trading in wildlife products.

GLOSSARY

balance of nature   a state of equilibrium among the various living things and forces in the natural world

baleen   substance similar to that found in fingernails, hooves, and horns that makes up the toothlike structures found in the mouths of certain whales; also called whalebone.

bounty   fee paid to a person for killing an animal that is viewed as unpopular or a nuisance

burrow   a hole or tunnel dug in the ground by an animal, used as a home and hiding place

captive breeding   the process of capturing animals from the wild and mating them in captivity in order to increase the species under protected conditions

carnivores   meat-eating creatures

coniferous   cone-bearing; for example, fir or pine trees

coterie   a small group of animals that are in frequent social contact

crossbreeding   mating of animals of different species or subspecies that produces mixed offspring

echolocation   process used by certain animals, such as bats, to sense their position in space and to locate other animals and objects by means of reflected sounds

ecosystem   an ecological community, along with its environment, viewed as a unit

endangered   an animal or a plant that is so few in number that it is in danger of becoming extinct

extinct   no longer in existence

family   a group of related plants or animals; in classification systems, family falls between order and genus in identifying living things

fertile   capable of reproducing

forage   plants or grasses eaten by grazing animals

habitat   area in which an organism normally lives and grows

hibernate   to sleep or remain inactive during periods of cold weather

hybrid   mixed breed that occurs when two different subspecies of animals mate and bear young

inbred   the result of inbreeding, or reproduction by closely related plants or animals

keratin   fibrous protein material found in the outer layer of fingernails, horns, and hooves

keystone species   a species that plays a fundamental role in maintaining the plants and animals in an ecosystem

midden   layers of seeds, tree cones, fungi, and other plants, stored by squirrels to be eaten during wintertime

order   a group of related animals or plants

parasites   tiny creatures, such as ticks or mites, that feed on larger animals, sucking their blood

predator   an animal that hunts other animals for food

range   geographical area in which an animal can be found

raptor   bird of prey (such as falcon, hawk, eagle)

sonar   a system that depends upon reflected sound waves to locate animals and objects underwater

species   distinct kinds of individual plants or animals that have common traits and share a common name

subspecies   a smaller group of plants or animals within a particular species

threatened   animals or plants that are in danger of extinction in a part of their range

INDEX